The Step Mom Syndrome

By Dawn Witt Denny

Dedication

I'd like to thank and recognize the following people: My husband, Steve, for his love, encouragement, and support on this book. My mother and father, Shirley and Gerry Witt, for their unconditional love and many, many prayers. My brother, Todd, who always encourages me to stand up. Lucas' stepfather, Gunnar, for his encouragement, understanding and honesty. Gunnar's mother, Rose, for her countless letters and gifts. And, of course, Lucas, who understands how hard it is for everyone to be a part of a blended family, and how each of us is right *and* wrong, and worthy of forgiveness and love.

Most of all, thank you to Jesus Christ, for His love and strength. May any and all glory be to God.

Table of Contents

Chapter 1: Defining the Step Mom Syndrome

A four year engagement went by quickly, as I tried to convince myself that having "the other woman" in my life for many years was "okay". Most step moms feel that way. When we marry someone who has been previously married, we realize that the first wife will be an active part of our lives for a long time.

I am described by friends as strong and confident. I went into marriage truly believing that the ex and I would not only get along, but that we would be friends! Stop laughing! I really did believe this! I based this on not having major conflicts with many people growing up. I like people, and thought this trait would benefit me as a step mom, and as a wife-in-law, as some people call the ex-wife and wife.

I wasn't expecting to fall into a painful depression after I slowly became the victim of lies and exaggerations by my step son. I had seen this happen to the step dad, and yet, I foolishly never thought it would happen to me.

So, after a four year engagement, and a ten plus year marriage, I found myself raising my stepson for six years - mostly on my own - and suddenly this strong and confident woman had turned into a bitter, angry, sad woman who frequently wanted to escape this turmoil and what felt like constant conflict!

My husband, Steve, and I went through three bouts of marriage counseling, individual therapy, and many, many, many bible studies.

I don't say this lightly - it is only because of the grace of Jesus Christ that our marriage survived, and now, thrives.

The ex did her best to turn Steve against me. So did my step son. So did my in laws. And suddenly, there was a time when I was so angry inside at people choosing to hate me - just because I was the "wicked stepmother" - that my bad attitudes also turned into actions. At that point, I exploded! I lied and I yelled, and I made a decision to actively hurt those people who I felt had deliberately hurt me. Many step mothers say they have experienced the same explosion.

I suddenly found myself looking in the mirror wondering who in the world I had become??? This was not me! I knew this! This was a person that Satan had tried to destroy. And my own self pity had helped him along the way.

But God is the god of redemption, and one day, when I was FAR from ready, he awakened me at night and encouraged me to write down what was happening. That's what this is.

I believe God wants to use this study to show step moms victory where they only see defeat. And that he wants to save marriages that seem hopeless.

It was that day that God started healing my wounded heart. Two years later, I found myself with a finished bible study, and started teaching it to step moms at Lakeview Church in Indianapolis.

Every single step mom who took part in the study, and every single step mom who chose to read it on their own time - says they went through similar circumstances, and felt completely defeated.

We can change the names and dates and circumstances, but the emotions and feelings were identical.

The feeling that their marriages could never possibly survive was always there.

The feeling that their husband was not "protecting them" was there.

The feeling, most of all, that we were wearing a target for everyone's anger and hatred - WOW, was that there!

I call it the Step Mom Syndrome.

Compare it to other medical syndromes like Down Syndrome or Chronic Fatigue Syndrome. Doctors recognize similar patterns and characteristics. Then, diagnosed, a person must identify it, learn from it, and live with it. Many live victoriously with their syndromes. We can, too.

But first, we need to understand that this is NOT something we "simply have to deal with".

Webster-Merriam's collegiate dictionary defines a syndrome as a group of signs and symptoms that occur together and characterize **a particular abnormality or condition OR** a set of concurrent things (as emotions or actions) that usually form an identifiable pattern Think about that as a step mom:

A group of symptoms that characterize a particular condition (remarriage to a man with children), and form an identifiable pattern (what step moms experience).

We do not go into marriage, thinking, "This is going to be a great *first* marriage!" We don't start a family thinking, "This is going to be a great *few* years……. until I leave and start again with someone else."

We get married, expecting to and hoping to *stay* married - and we have children - planning to raise them ourselves.

And yet, we find ourselves "suddenly **step moms**" - raising someone else's kids, being criticized on every move we make. We are in an abnormal condition!

Many step moms say "normal" moms don't have to listen to anywhere close to the amount of criticism step moms have to listen to - the in laws, the ex, the step children, their own husband - everybody has to have their say, right?

If we make a mistake, it never seems to disappear - and if we do something right, we can be perceived as trying to outdo the "real" mom - we often feel as though we just can't win!

There is a definite set of emotions or actions that follow a pattern to create the Step Mom Syndrome.

I've met so many step moms and after hearing their stories, it's amazing how the *facts* might be different but the *feelings* are the same, and the battles we face are shockingly similar. As divorce continues to shatter more and more homes, more and more step moms are created. And now, more than ever before, more step moms are the primary parent raising their step children. This causes a lot of conflict, a lot of grief, a lot of pain, but that's what we are going to stop in our own lives.

Here are some stories from some step moms:

Leslie is a step mom to two children. Her husband recently gained custody of the two children, making Leslie the full time caregiver. She says when she and her husband plan an evening out, and the ex is supposed to have visitation with the children, she deliberately cancels at the last minute. Leslie believes this is to interfere with the plans she has.

Carolyn is a step mom to a 7 year old boy. Her husband's ex has custody, so they have visitation. When visitation comes around, Carolyn's husband is usually working and that leaves Carolyn to pick up the child, shuttle him around, and many times, take him to doctor's appointments, or sporting events. Sometimes her husband shows up late - sometimes he misses them altogether. But she, the step mom, is there. She says no matter what she does, her in laws hate her, and make comments to her husband, including things like, "Tell her she's not Chris' mother."

Kelly's husband has custody of his two sons. His ex shows up unannounced and early for visitation. Kelly's husband tells her over the phone that the children are not to be allowed to leave with their mother until the court appointed time. Kelly respects her husband's decision, refuses to let the children go, and the ex parks in front of the house, staring at the house for a full two hours.

Jineane has a teenage step daughter. She's convinced the girls hates her. Jineane takes her to buy a dress for her high school graduation, and spends a fortune on the dress of the step daughter's choice, trying to please her. The teenager wears the beautiful dress in the car to graduation, disappears into a bathroom, and reappears wearing another dress altogether, giving Jineane a self satisfied look.

Kelli says report cards never seem to go back and forth between households. If her step kids are visiting their mom and it's report card time, the report doesn't make it to their house - not even a copy.

Joyce says her husband's ex never returns clothes the kids are wearing when they go to visit their mom. Sometimes, she says, she even sends a listing of the kids' clothes, hoping the mom might send all the clothes back.

Here are the symptoms we step moms experience. They can break us, and they can be heart breaking, and they lead to the step mom syndrome.

Symptoms:

1 - **Blind Hope** - The Honeymoon phase - The feeling that, "I can do this! I am woman!" (Usually prior to marriage.) Let's face it, you probably never doubted that you would be victorious even before you were "officially" the step mother, right? Your husband as your fiancé has been nothing short of wonderful, your soon to be step children love you, and the ex has been nice to you. What can possibly go wrong???

2 - **Sudden Shock/Confusion**: This occurs when you endure the first conflict after marriage. You were possibly surprised at your husband's response, shocked at your step child's involvement, feeling your boundaries breached by the ex's involvement. Lots of sudden happenings that cause us to feel a lack of control, lost, suddenly confused and a bit worried.

My Sudden Shock Symptom was all about toothpaste. Yes, toothpaste. Lucas had lived with us for about a week. He was 12. I was making breakfast, and he came in, walking around the house, brushing his teeth. I told him to brush his teeth in the bathroom so the toothpaste wouldn't drop all over the house. Lucas looked at me as though that order was so cruel that he could not believe it. And so did my husband. And then the story went to Lucas' mom, and all three of them just couldn't believe how mean I was.

This was about the time I started to think, uh-oh, if they are mad at me for small rules like this, what in the world is going to happen with big stuff?!

3 - **The Victim Phase**: In this phase, you feel like a victim. You feel cornered at times, You feel all three of them attack you with words to your face, words behind your back. Most step moms, like me, had never had this turmoil in their lives, so they are completely unprepared in how to handle this. It's new and it's deeply painful. This leads to:

4 - **Disillusionment** sets in nearly simultaneously with the Victim phase - I think this happens within one to two years of marriage, as we realize the attacks are going to continue - the step children lying or stretching the truth, your husband not really sure whether he should believe you or his child(ren), and the ex and what seems like her *need* to not approve of you.

5 - **Isolation** - we start to feel as though we are the ONLY person who has ever gone through something like this. We convince ourselves that "normal moms" just can't relate to what we are going through. We may try to talk to friends who are moms but not step moms, and hear suggestions that also leave us feeling **alienated**. We start to realize that being a mom and a step mom and two VERY different things. We begin to keep more inside, not wanting to talk about it, but still feeling very hurt inside.

6 - **Depression, Anger, A Loss of our Self- Esteem** - This sneaks up on us. When we see our friends in "normal marriages", "normal families", we start to see the grass as so much greener. We may start to question whether we ruined our lives by entering into this marriage. We start to consider leaving. We get very, very angry at the step child and his/her actions that seem to be "out to get us", the wedge it's put in our marriage, and the attacks on us by the ex. We start to lash out and lash back - you might see a viciousness within yourself that you didn't realize was there. This is when our attitudes turn into actions that we never thought were possible!

7 - **Self pity, feeling a Lack of Protection** - As our husbands struggle with what they are supposed to do, we feel unprotected. This breeds bitterness toward our men, anger toward our step children, and the ex. We begin to assign blame to one or all three.

8 - **Decision time** - This is when we choose - we either leave or we stand up and roll up our sleeves. Guess which one God wants you to do!

There are struggles every single step mom faces and we need to learn to get through it the godly way.

There's a reason God allowed you to be a step mom. He loves you, and He KNEW you could do it!!!

To get started, let's look inward.

Let's examine the emotions:

Do you:

1) Feel angry at your husband, your step child, your step children, the ex?
2) Feel sadness/sorrow/depression at situations you have endured?
3) Feel isolated, at times as though you are the only one going through this?
4) Feel your friends who are not step moms, but "just moms" have it easier and better, and that they can't understand?
5) Feel the desire to escape?
6) Feel attacked by the ex, by your step child or step children, and even your husband?
7) Feel a lack of protection from your husband?
8) Feel manipulated by the ex, your husband, or the step child?
9) Do you feel taken advantage of?
10) Do you ever not feel appreciated?

Circle all of the above that you have felt, and then make a list of the other emotions you have felt since becoming a step mother:

_____
_____
_____
_____
_____
_____

Now, let's look at the actions that could be described as a pattern:

Do you:

1) Lash out at your step children after these emotions we just discussed surface?
2) Lash out at your husband?
3) Hold grudges?
4) Remember past sins, and list them for the ex, the step child, the husband?
5) With-hold affection - not hug the child when you ought to - or ignore your husband's needs as a way to punish him?
6) Do you with-hold encouragement and positive reinforcement?
7) Do you intentionally miss activities the step child/ step children are involved in?
8) Do you sometimes try to "out mom" the biological mom?
9) Do you remind your husband of his past mistakes?

Circle the ones that pertain to you, and then list other actions you have taken since becoming a step mother.

_____

_____

_____
_____
_____
_____
_____

Have you seen the following occur in your household?

1) Your step child lying to the ex or to your husband about you?
2) You lying to your husband about the step child?
3) Your husband believing you are "harder" on the step child than on your own children?
4) Your husband buying expensive gifts for the child in an effort to win him/her over?
5) The ex attacking you verbally, either to the step child or to your husband?
6) Your in laws attacking you verbally over their opinion of your treatment of the step child?

Circle the ones that pertain to you, and then write other scenarios present in your household in the blank:

_____
_____
_____
_____
_____
_____

I've seen many step moms, including myself, quite unforgiving toward themselves. We're surrounded with people who "loved" us, but wanted to remind us of our failures quite often. Pastor Joel Osteen preached one day on people reminding us of our past sins. Paraphrasing his words, he said something like this, "If you have expressed genuine remorse to the person you wronged, and confessed your sins to God, then God has wiped it out! He no longer has a record of that. So if someone is accusing you of being "that type of person" or reminding you of what you've done, they're not speaking for God. So who are they speaking for?"

I LOVE THAT! Satan is the accuser. Not God. When you are forgiven, you don't have to be forgiven over and over and over by a person for the same sin.

Now that all the junk is out, let's look at what we want:
Do you want:

1) Respect from your husband, your step child, the ex?
2) Fewer conflicts in your home?
3) To feel appreciated?
4) To feel loved?

Circle what you want, and then list what else your heart desires:

_____

_____

_____

_____

_____

_____

Chapter 2: Understanding the People who Hurt you:

Identification and Understanding:

God expects us to be wise enough to understand people in a deeper way. I am in no way condoning bad behavior, but I believe if we understand more behind a person and their thinking, we can identify what their true motives are. Then, we can learn a better way to deal with them.

Consider the relationships in your life as a step mom.

* *The Step Mom and the Step child/step children:*

Where are they coming from? They want their parents together. They have to tell every story twice - once to your household, once to the other household. That could be irritating and tiring! They are confused. They lie - sadly, all kids lie, and will continue to unless parents help them change that behavior. We need to understand that this is usually a cry for attention, not a deliberate attack upon us.

They will lash out most at the person they feel most secure about. In my case, this was me. We learned in counseling that Lucas was lashing out more at me because he truly believed he could come back to me, apologize, and that I would accept him back into my circle. He felt rejected by his father, Steve, because of the divorce, and felt rejected by his mother, Ann, because she sent him to live with us. Hearing this made me look my situation in a much more godly manner. That's you, too!!! Try to pick apart what hurts your stepchild, and it can help you understand and love him much better.

When Lucas was a teenager, and would come home from school, I was the one there for him. Steve travels quite a bit, and Lucas' mom lived out of state. I had two toddlers at the time, so my time and attention was spread pretty thin. Lucas really needed more attention than anyone gave him, and this caused him to be angry. He wanted to come home to at least one of his parents, and he often didn't. This caused him to lash out at me quite often. It also caused me to develop an irritation with him, not wanting my little ones to witness his outbursts of verbal or physical anger. This also caused me to be quite aggravated with the ex for sending him to live with us, and at my husband for being gone so much. I felt everyone could hang up the phone and go on with their lives, but I had to raise their son alone! I became quite resentful of what I perceived as my husband and his ex wife "dumping" their kid on me when it was no longer convenient for them to raise him.

I needed to realign my thinking out of this world, and into God's realm. God had me there for a reason. I needed to listen to Him, not the world.

One of Kelly's stepson's has attention deficit disorder. When the school called and requested a parent chaperone him in class for two weeks, the mom refused. Dad had to work. Guess who did it? Kelly was there for the full two weeks. She also struggled with the stepson's behavior affecting her two children. Unfortunately, bad behavior is much easier to mimic than good behavior. Kelly could have been angry. Instead, she chose to think of her stepson, and the bigger picture. If she's there for him, he sees it. Her kids see it. The ex sees it. Her worth is skyrocketing because she did what no one else would. Be there for your step child when no one else is. Do it with a godly heart.

* *The Step Mom and Her Husband:*

He's the HUB. The one who hears it from you, the kids, the ex. Everyone has their own version of every story, and every person believes their version is the right one!!! We need to understand that hearing the same story from so many sources is quite draining on our man. He is physically and emotionally exhausted many times when he gets around to "our" side of the story. He wants you to feel loved and protected, and he feels angry at himself when he realizes he's not protected you in the way you've expected.

Some men get so overwhelmed with this role that they disengage. One step mom was present while the ex was criticizing her to her husband. She waited for her man to defend her, but he simply did not respond at all. This encouraged the ex to continue her verbal attack, reinforced the ex's feelings about the step mom, and belittled the step mom's authority to the ex and to the step child. None of it was intended by the Dad, but he "couldn't take it any more" and he shut down. That left the stepmother feeling violated and unprotected.

Lucas always tried to speak to each parent privately. This was the way he would control the communication. He could twist some things around to Steve, and make Steve wonder if Lucas was telling the truth. He would also do this to his mother about his step father. And when the step father requested a meeting with all 5 of us together to compare some stories, Lucas wanted no part of it. This was a good tactic to slow down the lying and manipulation.

* *The Mom and the Step Mom:*

The ex: She's watching you, another woman, raise and love her child. She's jealous. She feels guilty. She doesn't want to approve of anything you do because she's afraid that would just reinforce her insecurity that she failed as a mother. She probably feels that if she likes you it means she is less of a mother, less of a woman. What I've seen is moms who are not raising their own children can be very insecure. They feel the world is labeling them a "bad mom". They feel they are failures.

In most cases, the mom develops a need to manipulate circumstances. This comes from feeling completely out of control. When Lucas and I would have silly disagreements on subjects like chores, there were plenty of times he started complaining to his mom about how "hard"

I was on him. This was quite convincing, but she also "wanted" to believe that there was no earthly way I was doing a good job. So, her response to Lucas was to agree with him, which encouraged him to be even more disrespectful. She would then call my husband under the guise of "not wanting to start trouble but...", or use a phrase like, "I'm just being honest...", or "maybe she is too hard on him". All of these were ways to manipulate Steve into thinking his wife was not being kind to his son. And they were the same tactics Steve used when Lucas lived with her! Lucas would tell tragic stories of his step dad chasing him with a hammer, and tackling him to the ground and hitting him. Whatever lies Lucas could muster, the biological parent wanted to believe Lucas, and that gave them power to believe they were "better" than the step parents.

There are going to be many times we need to look at situations and try to understand *why* all of these people are acting or reacting the way they are. If we try to understand, *we* might be slower to react, and therefore, we might handle it better!

* *The Step Mom and HERSELF:*

We are trying to do it right, trying not to step on people's toes, trying to be protected, trying to be loved. We are the perfectionists in the mix. Hard on our man, hard on our step children, hard on the ex, and hardest on ourselves. What WE need to understand is that we need to give ourselves a break! What I've seen in doing this for 14 years so far, is that the step kids, the exes, the husbands - they all give themselves a break. And yet, *We* do not. We have to find a way to get there, and that is part of the goal of this study.

We want the step children to understand that we love them, and we wish they had the maturity to understand that we are really trying.

We want our husbands to defend us always, and we want them to trust our mothering no matter what the step children or the ex say.

I wanted the ex to understand that raising a hormonal teenager along with two toddlers is tough! We wish she would grant us a chance to make mistakes but make up for them!

Now, read those three last points, and forget about it! I had to wake up and realize:

My husband was confused. My step son was lonely for his mother. The ex was absolutely ravaged with guilt about sending her son away, and because of that, she needed to hate me in order to deal with what she had done.

Phew!

Now, I needed to heal myself with God's amazing grace, and figure out how I could give Him glory in such a mess.

The first thing we are going to do is dwell on a verse this week - Psalm 57:4 "I am in the midst of lions. I lie among ravenous beasts - men whose teeth are spears and arrows, whose tongues are sharp swords."

Here's why I chose that verse to begin this study: My Life Application Bible says this in the notes referring to the above verse, "When confronted with verbal attacks, *the best defense is simply to be quiet* and praise God, realizing that our confidence is in His love and faithfulness. In times of great suffering, don't turn inward to self-pity or outward to revenge, but upward to God."

It's human nature to want to grab tightly onto the idea of revenge, or wallow in the poor me attitude when things go wrong. But we are SO MUCH MORE than simply human nature! We are God's beloved.

When you feel defeated, read Psalm 64, and put your name in the first line, "Hear me, (your name) O God, as I voice my complaint, protect my life from the threat of the enemy."

Remember as you raise this psalm to the Lord, the enemy is not your stepchild, your husband, not even the ex. The enemy is Satan. ***<u>You can have victory by choosing when to pray it and when to say it!</u>*** Your words can be life building or life draining - listen closely to your mouth this week, "For out of the overflow of the heart, the mouth speaks." Luke 6:45

Rent the movie "Step Mom" this week, especially if you haven't seen it. Here's what I want you to look for:

If we are honest with ourselves, most of us as step moms can relate to both women, Julia Roberts and Susan Sarandon, and I'd even guess that most of us LIKE both characters in the movie. It's easy for us to sit in the theater and like them both, and laugh at the mistakes both of them are making. And it's easy for us to understand both sides, as we watch the movie.

That's basically where we need to be - *understanding* BOTH sides.

There's one point when the son tells his mom that he will hate his step mom if his mother wants him to hate her. And that is the message many of our children are getting. In the movie, the step mom is also fervently trying to defend herself over and over to the kids and the ex and to her husband. She is often quite critical of the mother. We can see that many times Roberts is exasperated with her role, and it's easy for us to relate because step moms get weary!!

When we objectively look at that movie, we should be mature enough to see that BOTH women are truly trying to do what's best for the kids (even when they are going about it wrong), and in the step mother's case, she is also trying to do the best for her man (that is an important part for us to remember).

Yes, it's a Hollywood movie, so of course, everyone loves everybody else at the end. But watch it with a different attitude - an attitude of understanding, of relating to both characters and try to put yourself IN both spots. Try to watch this alone so no one is explaining to you how you SHOULD feel.

Points to Ponder this week:
Part 1 of 3: The Lesson of Silence.

There was a church bulletin board posted. It read, "Silent and Listen have the same letters." Step moms are not meek people. We are strong by the very fact that we *chose* to marry a man with kids. We believed we could handle it. We believed we could do it. But at some point, most of us reach a point where the Enemy has needled us enough that we say - at least to ourselves - "This is not what I signed up for!"

This week, we are going to practice *actively being quiet*. Do not turn this into a lesson on the "silent treatment", or remind your husband or step child that you are "not talking". This is not the goal.

The goal is to seriously listen. This is hard for me! It took me 5 years to learn that I needed to shut up! And it hit me when God allowed me to be so worn down that I didn't have the strength to argue back.

I was sitting at the kitchen table. It was 2005, the night before I was supposed to drive 5 hours to meet my husband's ex, and deliver my stepson. My stepson was livid, filled with rage, and I was his target. I had asked him to vacuum the SUV, and then given him tips on how to do it right (my "big mouth effect"). He then retaliated by calling his mom and telling her I was refusing to drive him halfway to her the following day. She called my husband, who asked me if that was true. The lie was revealed, and yet, I was the bad guy in my stepson's eyes.

I never said I wouldn't drive him, but I had angered my stepson in my "directions" on how to vacuum a car, and then my husband desperately wanted to believe his son, so I was the target.

I sat at the table, closed mouthed, and listened. I listened to Lucas tell me how awful I made his life, and how he wished I wasn't there. I heard my husband criticize my way of doing things, saying he could "understand" Lucas' point of view.

Now, don't feel sorry for me - this is after 5 years of me very much taking part in such arguments - and throwing daggers back - quite sharp daggers.

The difference this time is I had spent the day in the Word, and had God in my heart and mind - much different than just having myself in my mind and heart. I stood up after the verbal beating, and said only, "I love you both. I have made mistakes in the past. But I am doing the best I know how. I love you." Then I went up to bed. TOTAL SILENCE IN THAT KITCHEN!!!!!

The next morning, I got up to a two page heartfelt letter from my stepson. It started with, "Dawn, I can't sleep because I am so ashamed of the things I said to you. You didn't deserve any of it." He then went on to list so many things he appreciated - my doing his schedule, making sure he was signed up for everything on time, doctors appointments, dentists, etc. I have kept it to this day.

My husband? I woke up to a tearful man who regretted his involvement, filled with godly remorse, hoping I would forgive him.

God blessed me with that response from both of them because I was obedient! I kept still. I listened. I did not fight back.

This week, let's dwell on verses that encourage us to be still and listen - let's listen to God, to our husbands, to our children and step children. Let's DECIDE not to react, but rather love in our attitudes and our LACK of words.

Isaiah 30:15 says "This is what the Sovereign Lord, the Holy One of Israel, says: "In repentance and rest is your salvation, **in quietness and trust is your strength**."

Grab a pen and scribble down some honest answers over the next few pages.

Think back to the last time you adamantly defended yourself to your step child or your husband.

_____

_____

_____

_____

Was their response open to your feelings and thoughts? Or were they closed off to hearing you?

_____

_____

_____

_____

Do you now think that had you handled it in a calm and quieter fashion, you may have been heard? Why or why not?

_____

_____

_____

_____

Read the last part again: "….In quietness and trust is your strength."

Quietness - It's not us shouting about the great job we are doing, or listing for them all we've done (I am certainly guilty of that!) It's doing it with a quiet and gentle heart with PURE motives. Do it for LOVE - the love of God and the child and your man - not because you are keeping a running tally.

Write out Zephaniah 3:17:

_____

_____

_____

_____

"He will quiet you with His love." Write that down on a piece of paper that you can put somewhere to read each day this week. How beautiful. Quietness doesn't equate to weakness. It equates to the absolute knowledge that *we* are not in control, but rather the Lord is. It's not about how much you talk. It's about your heart.

He can quiet out pain, our heart, our longings…. And he quiets us with his love.

Now read 1 Timothy 2:11. "A woman should learn in quietness and full submission."

I believe this means we should fully submit to God, to Christ. I believe it means we are to be so involved in his Word that we think on it night and day, and that we submit to God - NOT our earthly desires to be first, to be recognized, to be number one. And when we learn true submission to our Father, we can act on true submission to our husbands.

In our step mom scenario, this means at the most difficult times, for us to hold our tongues, pray for our husbands, and encourage our husbands to parent without our interference, at times. Notice I said, at times - more on that later.

Your reward? Here it is! Just like the "morning after" that I described after the verbal attack, I was blessed with witnessing true remorse by Lucas and Steve.

1 Peter 3:4 talks about a woman's beauty: "It should be that of your inner self, the unfading beauty of a gentle and quiet spirit, which is of great worth in God's sight."

This week, if something happens to disrupt your peace, stay quiet, and immediately go to the Word. Read and re-read these passages. Do not state your case, or say your piece. Try with all of your might to wait 12 to 24 hours, and then if you truly feel you need to say something to your husband, do so in a manner that you believe Christ would use to speak to him. Loving, calm, gentle. Few words but words that build, not drain.

Do not give your opinion to your step children on any conflict or situation. Love them as your would your own, but this week, lovingly separate yourself from putting your opinions out there!

Come back to this section and write out what happened and how you handled it, what you did right and what you could have done better:

_____
_____
_____
_____
_____
_____
_____
_____
_____
_____

Luke 8: 21 And Jesus said, **"My mother and brothers are those who hear God's word and put it into practice."**

Part 2 of 3: Deliberate Encouragement

Satan cannot remain in the presence of joy. He can't take it. The second he enters your household and begins making trouble, identify it. Identify him. Your step children, your husband, your husband's ex - they are NOT the enemy, although most of us have pointed an accusatory finger at all of them. I know I have, and I was desperately wrong.

Satan is the one who causes trouble, and who stirs it up. Yes, we make choices and we decide how to act and react, but we need to be aware that this is ALL a spiritual battle.

Ephesians 6:12 says "For our struggle is not against flesh and blood, but against the rulers, against the authorities, against the powers of this dark world and against the spiritual forces of evil in the heavenly realms."

We need to reign in our anger toward people, and realize who is causing the conflict. How do we fight the Devil? Easy. We DECIDE to, and we do so by CHOOSING to remain the presence of joy, where he cannot stay.

Step 1: Don't get too busy to read your Word daily. This is the first thing Christians "put off" when the Devil successfully distracts them with problems. Read the Psalms. They will show you the trials people went through - the feelings they battled - just as we do. Read on until you find one that encourages you. God will nudge you along until you are there. Let Him lead you.

Step 2: Worship Music! Forget the top 40. You need to have worship songs in your heart, head and soul so that when you awaken in the middle of the night, they are the tunes your mind is playing, not a rock and roll jingle. These minister to your spirit, even in your sleep, just as the secular songs can open portals to negativity without us consciously realizing it.

Step 3: OPEN YOUR BIG MOUTH!

What? I thought your last lesson was teaching me to keep my mouth closed. Yes, it was. Now, I am telling you to open it with deliberate encouragement. DELIBERATE, PURE, MEANINGFUL ENCOURAGEMENT.

I have seen this work wonders with my step son, after years of me messing it up. Let me share with you the worst thing I ever said to my dear Lucas. In a typical teenage argument, he was reaching for anything to get me riled up. He started throwing out the "My mom does this and that better than you...." and, even though I knew deep down he was only trying to hurt me, I lashed back, "Well, your mother doesn't want you." To this day, I find myself struggling over forgiving myself for saying that.

Here he was, sent to live with us at age 12, seeing his mom 30 to 50 days a year, and of course, who wouldn't feel rejected? And I threw that out..... Ouch.

I remember telling Lucas' youth pastor that I had said that, and that Lucas had then spit at me. Instead of being shocked at Lucas, the youth pastor gently told me, "You'll have to genuinely tell him you're sorry for saying that." He was so right, and I did.

When I did apologize to Lucas, he shocked me with maturity, and also told me how he regretted saying so many things he didn't mean, and also told me he knew I loved him, and that he realized he was deliberately provoking me because HE was angry inside (like many kids of divorce!).

I love when God turns bad situations into good life lessons!

I learned then to deliberately encourage in an effort to build Lucas up and actively make sure he felt loved.

Here's what we are going to do together for the rest of this week. Make a list for your husband, and each of your step children. Write down 5 positive things you can say to them EACH day that you see them if they only visit you, or EVERY day if they live with you. Things like, "Your hair looks great." or "That color looks really good on you." Build up their self esteem.

Did they have a test? Ask them how it went, and if it went badly, don't suggest studying harder. Say something like, "Would you like me to study with you for the next one?" Or tell them about a test you thought you nailed but ended up bombing when you were in school.

You know what they like to eat - have it in the house in a prominent location and tell them you bought it just for them because you *remembered* they like it.

Lucas loves my cooking, and I know my beef stroganoff is his favorite, so I love to cook it for him when he's going through a rough spot.

Do something they won't expect! I printed a picture of Lucas' mother from 27 years ago when she was at her bridal shower. She looked great, and was clearly beaming with excitement. I printed it for Lucas, and put it in his room, telling him what it was from and that I thought he'd like to have it. That reinforced to him that I was "trying", and I was thinking of HIM.

For your husband - write him a love note. Send him a cookie gram or flowers to work. Bake something for him to take to work so others will rave about your baking and how lucky he is! Buy him a CD. Do something and remember to SAY 5 things to him throughout the day, too.

Remember how we learned our husbands are the "HUB"? They hear it from us, from our step children, from their ex. Our men are the central office, so to speak. So their weariness is much greater than ours, and it's much more that he holds in!

Express to him this week that you realize it must be difficult for him to hear so many different things and so many different complaints from so many venues. Ask him how you can help him ease that burden, and try, try, try to comply! When my husband is going through trials with his ex and his son, the last thing he needs sometimes is my opinion, and yet, it sometimes the first thing I offered!

He told me last year, "I just need to NOT talk about it. I feel like I have to talk about this non-stop... with my ex, my son, my parents, and you." I promised to try, and just a month ago, another issue/conflict came up. I tried to put this action of non-action to the test.

It worked! Steve has commended me numerous times for allowing him to deal with the situation with no interference from me, and I found an amazing peace with the Lord in trusting God, rather than myself, in controlling the situation!

Deliberately encourage your household this week. Choose it and do it. You will be a blessing to all of them, and in turn, ***you will be blessed for your deliberate obedience to God's word.***

Part 3 of 3:
Choosing ACTIVE Forgiveness

As step moms, we are more often than not victims of terrible verbal abuse. Verbal attacks from the ex wife, from our own husbands, and from our step children. And, unfortunately, we are sometimes the victim of lies.

The storybooks don't help. Hansel and Gretel's step mother tried to kill them. Snow White's step mother tried to have her killed. Cinderella's step mother made her a slave. Children grow up learning to hate step mothers! We read it to them with smiles on our faces!! And where are the dads in these stories? We are always to assume they are weak, and that they don't stick up for their children. They are absent.

This week, I want you to practice active forgiveness. You know what you are harboring and refusing to forgive. This is sin. We all do it. One of my biggest challenges is to forgive people when they wrong me and then refuse to apologize. It's tough!

Recently, I was the victim of a lie by my husband's ex and her husband. They took this lie to friends of ours, colleagues of ours, and my in laws. When I found out about it, I was so mad that I vowed to myself and to my husband - that I would not speak to them or forgive them until they apologized to me. Well, a year went by and that apology never came! Are you shocked? No - neither was I.

Then Lakeview Church Pastor Ron Bontrager preached one Sunday about the joy in forgiveness. You see, I was choosing to limit my joy in Christ by choosing to be irritated at a lie - a lie, I should add, that no one believed. Not one person. All who heard it told me about it and then reinforced to me that they knew it was not true. That was a CLEAR blessing from God, protecting me from a lie! And instead of rejoicing in that, I looked upon myself and CHOSE TO SIN by not forgiving.

I'm telling you one of the hardest things for me to do is forgive without an apology - and when I started to think about it, I felt like a fool. Here my God was, blessing me with an honor of having every single person believe in me, and honor me, and I was choosing bitterness.

So I told my husband, I am going to say every day to myself and to God, "I forgive them. I forgive them. I FORGIVE THEM. And, Lord, forgive me for NOT forgiving them immediately."

This active forgiveness almost immediately relieved a burden from me. I nearly felt a physical change in my shoulders relaxing and a breath of relief coming from my mouth. God will indeed help us forgive when we give it to him and ask him to teach us how to, and we speak it from our mouths - for the scripture says, "Out of the overflow of the heart, the mouth speaks." I firmly believe that if we speak it, we will build it into our hearts.

Whatever you are holding on to - insults, lies, accusations, jealousy - toward the ex, your step child, your husband - say out loud "Lord, I forgive (put their name here)"

Trust the Lord. He will make you FEEL that forgiveness and it will free you to focus on Christ and who you are supposed to be through Him.

I made that decision to forgive with no apology based a bit on my fear of the Lord. When I thought about it, and standing in front of Him, and trying to explain to him why I certainly had the right to feel wronged, and be mad….. I could imagine him say, "And even though I blessed you with an immediate blessing protecting you from that lie, you have disappointed me, my child. You rejected my power and love for you and tried to dictate how the situation should be handled. Your job, Dawn, is to forgive. I have the rest."

Let go of trying to force that person you are upset with into doing what you see as the right thing.

God was trying to teach me to **forgive as he commands** us all to do. He doesn't say, "Hey, do not forgive until you receive an apology." We are expected to "confess our sins to one another."

But don't be the person pointing that out.

Be the one demonstrating active forgiveness without the apology.

James 5:16 says, "Therefore confess your sins to each other and pray for each other so that you may be healed. The prayer of a righteous man is powerful and effective."

1 John 2:9 says, "Anyone who claims to be in the light but hates his brother is still in the darkness."

For months, I was in the darkness in God's eyes because I was choosing to be angry at my husband's ex. I felt wronged and wanted that silly, all-important apology. The second I gave it to God, admitted the sin I had chosen, I was free! More importantly, I was forgiven!

It's not our job to tell others they need to apologize. Look, God knows everyone's actions, and everyone's motives behind their actions. We cannot make people act the way we want them to. We MUST do what GOD expects. And what God expects is simple, but difficult forgiveness….. And he expects us to act on it when no apology is anywhere close to our radar.

Read that 1 John scripture again. We want to live in the light, don't we? The moment I actively gave this to God, and spoke with my lips each day, I seriously felt differently. I felt clear, free. Blessings began to occur nearly immediately. Test this. Act upon forgiving the person you are struggling to forgive, and then write down the blessings you are seeing in this obedience to God.

I started to see it in my step son's behavior, his attitude. I said nothing about this decision to actively forgive, but when the phone rang, and it was his step father, I was nice and upbeat, giving the phone to Lucas. This was the positive example God wanted me to portray, not the martyristic approach to which I had been clinging. My husband also saw it. I explained what I had done wrong, in choosing to avoid forgiveness. This turned out to be a lesson for him, too!

God made me being wronged, right. He fixed it the second it came out of the mouths of those speaking it because he honored me with no one believing it. HE is in control. Let Him be.

Go away from this lesson in the fear of how big our God really is. Give Him that respect. Don't make excuses. Just forgive that person who lied about you, insulted you, treated you poorly. Whatever it is - identify what it is you are holding on to and daily say, "Lord, I forgive so and so for their sin. Help me to love them as you command."

He will help you.

Exodus 14:13-14

Do not be afraid. Stand still, and see the salvation of the Lord, which He will accomplish for you today....

The Lord will fight for you, and you shall hold your peace...

Chapter 3: The Sin Of Justification.

Most of us realize by this stage in our life that divorce is a sin. In Mark chapter 10, the Pharisees remind Jesus that Moses allowed a man to write a certificate of divorce and send his wife away. Verse 5 says Jesus told the Pharisees, *"It was because your hearts were hard that Moses wrote you this law. But at the beginning of creation God 'made them male and female'. 'For this reason a man will leave his father and mother and be united to his wife, and the two will become one flesh.' So they are no longer two, but one. Therefore what God has joined together, let man not separate."*

We are going to be restored by Christ, and if you listen to Him, he will show you how to restore your home, your heart, your marriage.

* Personal Accountability: (Out with the Old)

The first step in restoration is accountability. Have you ever noticed when someone tells you they are divorced, it's normally followed up with a story of how awful the ex spouse was? It's a rare person to take responsibility for a failed marriage, but it's a **mature** one! I had to confess that I had so much anger over being rejected by my husband's family that it built a temple of unforgiveness in my heart. And if I'm holding tightly to unforgiveness, I certainly can't hold on to Christ. We can choose one or the other, and whichever we choose will also determine whether we will choose victory or defeat.

We have to admit that a justification for divorce is wrong.

People have been justifying their actions and sins since Creation. Read Genesis 3:11-13. *"And he said, "Who told you that you were naked? Have you eaten from the tree that I commanded you not to eat from?" The man said, "The woman you put here with me - she gave me some fruit from the tree, and I ate it." Then the Lord God said to the woman, "What is this you have done?" The woman said, "The serpent deceived me, and I ate it."*

The blame game doesn't fly with God!

Eve had a choice. God gave us a very dangerous quality, and that is the power of choice. ***That is what dictates our maturity - the choices we make - especially the choices we make when NO ONE IS WATCHING.***

Eve's sin was forgiven by God, but there are still consequences to every sin. Just because we regret what we've done doesn't mean we no longer have to pay the price for our decisions.

Genesis 3:16 shows us that Eve's consequences would live **until this day**. *"To the woman, he said, "I will greatly increase your pains in childbearing; with pain you will give birth to children."*

Let me also say here I am not saying that I think anyone should stay in a marriage in which they are abused or in danger. That is not the lesson I am teaching. In those cases, I believe God has provided shelters and help and counseling for those victims. There are times when we have to be physically protected.

But we also need to look back on the behavioral patterns WE were following before we entered into such a relationship, identify them, confess them, heal them, and then use that experience to help others in similar situations.

THAT is how God uses each one of us to build his kingdom - He pulls us out of the fire, and expects us to turn around, reach back in, and pull someone else out, too.

Adam sinned willingly with Eve, and so God also punished him, Verses 17 -19, *"Cursed is the ground because of you; through painful toil you will eat of it all the days of your life. It will produce thorns and thistles for you, and you will eat the plants of the field. By the sweat of your brow you will eat your food until you return to the ground since from it you were taken; for dust you are and to dust you will return."*

Adam's sin of compliance, of not standing firm and following God's command to not eat from that tree, left him with consequences forever!

Be honest here: How did you last describe to someone the reason/justification for your divorce, or for your husband's divorce?

_____

_____

_____

_____

_____

_____

God understands that we all have the need to feel approval. But we get it wrong when we are trying to seek that through other people nodding their heads, saying, "Oh, you poor thing. Good thing you left."

I believe God is pleased when we say, "I made a mistake…." And then get to the part where God's power intervened in your thinking, in your heart!! We don't have to beat ourselves up but we need the confession to be sincere so God is well pleased with our honesty, and then practice saying it. Get the "God words" in your vocabulary. ***God can be glorified in our mistakes when we glorify Him and his restoration of us.***

Read 2 Kings chapter 10, verses 18 - 33.

Now look at Numbers 25:4 *The Lord said to Moses, "Take all the leaders of these people, kill them and expose them in broad daylight before the Lord, so that the Lord's fierce anger may turn away from Israel."*

You see, even though the Israelites believed God, they tolerated paganism, and soon it filtered into their rituals. They tolerated the idolatry, and began to worship Baal. The Israelites justified their actions because it supported the actions they wanted to pursue in their lives at the time. Sound familiar? I believe that is what we are doing as a society now with divorce. We love God, but we don't stand up against divorce the way we should, just as the Israelites didn't stand up against paganism the way they should have.

We have all done this at some point - convinced ourselves that a sin isn't "that bad".

What a dangerous game to play!

But this infuriated God, and God ordered the leaders teaching the paganism killed.

That scripture is so important! *We can follow God, and be blessed, and then still lose sight of Him, and again fall into habitual sin. We must not become tolerant of sin, or excuse it.*

In the same way, we must view divorce as sin, confess it and our responsibility to God, and then, **just as important** - accept his forgiveness!

It's just as wrong to dwell upon the sin as it is to ignore confronting it.

We cannot dictate what God will allow us to do just to justify what we want to do. I had a lady once tell me she left her husband for 6 weeks because she needed "time to think", and she was too angry to be in his presence. She then said she believed God "permitted" her to do that.

Ladies, that is absolutely not true, and that justification of separating a family is a lie from Satan, the Great Deceiver.

That is exactly the same thing the people of Israel did in the book of Kings! *You cannot act the way you want, and then "justify" it away by putting God's name in your explanation.* **You can call it whatever you want, but God calls it SIN.**

Most times, if you feel the need to present a lengthy explanation to someone about some action you have taken or something you have done, *that* should be your first clue that your heart and your motives were not in line with God's will. Jesus didn't fall all over himself explaining and justifying things the way we do. His explanations were loving, peaceful. Our explanations are shouted from the rooftops, sometimes even trying to convince ourselves - On the contrary, Christ KNEW, and KNOWS, and therefore, the son of God didn't have to shout anything to explain. His gentleness was strength. His calmness was proof.

You have a new house now. One was divided and fell. Your house will stand if you build it with Christ at the center. Christ says you are a new creation in Him - that means now - that means your marriage - that means the family you are now responsible for raising. *It doesn't mean there will not be trouble. It means God will be there every step of the way, and he WILL use everything for good. That's his promise.* HIS PROMISE. Read that aloud - His promise to me is Romans 8:28. *For I know that **everything** works together for good for those who love the Lord and who work according to His purpose.*

Do not listen to Satan and believe your marriage and family are doomed because you have married a divorced man, or that you were divorced and so you are cursed. There is a maturity that comes with recognizing, 1) yes, I sinned, 2) a true repentance NOT a justification, and then 3) a FULL spiritual cleansing where God makes us white as snow. As he says in Isaiah 1:18, *"Though your sins are like scarlet, they shall be as white as snow; though they are red as crimson, they shall be like wool."*

Listen to the rest in verse 19, *"If you are willing and obedient, you will eat the best from the land; but if you resist and rebel, you will be devoured by the sword."*

There's that choice thing, again. We can choose to obey, and receive blessings, or choose to do our own sinful thing, and face the sword.

It's easy to SAY what we should do, what we want to do, but it's a whole new ball game to make those right decisions when you have people in your own house who are expecting you to fail, hoping you will fail, and even encouraging you to fail. Ever feel like that? Most step moms have.

Now, finally, let's get back to facing our sin:

Write in the blank what you believe your sin was in the failure of your marriage, if you've been divorced.

_____
_____
_____
_____
_____
_____

Have you confessed it to Jesus?_____
If not, why not? _____

Let's take a moment to pray that our part will be revealed to us so that we can be cleansed. This also means forgiving ourselves. Let's give it to Christ and let Him love on us! This is the first step toward healing.

* Consequences to Sin:

Just as Eve tried to hide her sin, then justify it, and then blame the Serpent for tempting her, we do the same thing with our sins. Just as the Israelites tolerated paganism, we do the same thing in tolerating sin.

And *there are consequences to every sin.*

I believe the turmoil, the conflict, the feelings of "something is just not right" is a consequence of divorce. The legal battles in which no one is ever satisfied, the trying to "one up" the other parent with gifts, or trips, or time with the children. The feeling that one side needs to "stick it to the other", the trying to get the child on one side or the other. These are all behaviors that have developed after:

1) Someone chose to sin with a divorce.
2) There was justification and no remorse for this sin against God, and
3) Blame was evident - probably in both camps.

This leads to thought patterns of bitterness, anger, irritation, a want for revenge. This leads to talking about such things that give us an unsatisfied feeling. And, then, it leads to acting out on such behavior in an effort to "feel better", to "feel justified", to feel vengeance. This will not stop without God, without us reading His word every single day, admitting to Him our feelings, and asking Him to help us through it.

We need to:
Identify it.

Conquer it.
Learn from it.
Teach others how to do the same!

Claim your cleansing in Christ. I make it a habit each day to say, "Lord, cleanse my spirit." I do this because sometimes we allow our human nature to invade our spirit and we don't recognize it early enough.

Let Christ help you with this battle - he is your Commander!

When was the last time you prayed on your knees?

Get on your knees now, and pray out loud:

"Lord, Ezra 9:15 says: "O Lord, God of Israel, you are righteous! We are left this day as a remnant. Here we are before you in our guilt, though because of it not one of us can stand in your presence."

Lord, reveal to me my excuses, and my justifications. Wave them like a banner in front of my blind eyes so that I can identify and rid my myself of them. I cannot do this alone, Lord. Help me. Give me strength. I trust you. I adore you. I want to follow YOU, Lord, not my own selfish desires.

Help me to get the log out of my own eye, Lord, so that I can see clearly up to YOU. I know you love me, Lord, and I know you can turn around what I am grasping onto. Help me release what Satan has thrown into my path. Cast it into the fiery lake, and pull me up to your safety, the freedom that comes in following you, not me.

In the **mighty** name of Christ Jesus, Amen"

* Justifying Other Coveted Sin:

Maybe your coveted sin is not a divorce in your background, but your husband's. Do you justify all the reasons he ended the relationship?

Do you paint the ex as the worst person in the world, with no good qualities? That is judgment - is that your sin that you want to hold on to? Do you justify in your mind why it was okay for your husband and his wife to divorce?

After years of embracing it, I came to realize with God's help that I was living with coveted sin, a sin that I felt "belonged to me", and therefore I wanted to keep it. It was a huge barrier to my freedom in Christ and how close I could feel to him.

My coveted sin was feeling justified in being angry at the treatment I had received from my stepson, and my husband's ex, my in laws, and my own husband. The anger had become a part of me, and led me to do things to 'act out" against the injustice I felt in my heart. I honestly felt that I had the right to be upset that I wasn't treated absolutely perfectly in this odd situation!

What a joke!

It was years until I woke up one day, after attending so many Bible studies, and God so clearly told me to let it go, confess it to my husband, and start healing. The confession brought my man to tears. You see, he never intended me to ever feel angry at any of those people, and he, in fact, wanted to protect me from ever feeling that way. It broke his heart to hear that I had DECIDED to wave a banner over myself for years, proclaiming the VICTIM stance - "Oh, well, let me tell you the latest pain my husband's ex has caused, or how my stepson just spoke to me, or how my in laws just can't love me the way I'd like them to." Poor me... *__Every single time I thought it, every time I spoke it, every time I even felt it - I was choosing to sin.__*

I had to give that coveted sin to God so that I could be free. I truly felt a weight lifted off of me when I finally did that!

Some women covet that glass of wine, they can't live without it - it makes their difficult day "livable".

What do you covet that you know deep down is not pleasing God?

If we have a sin we love, a sin we covet, then we are justifying what we WANT to do, or we are justifying a thought pattern. That's what I was doing. I justified "feeling" like a victim, feeling I was treated badly by certain people. That became a thought pattern that I WANTED to keep. That was sin. God did not want me in bondage - he wanted me to admit those feelings to Him, give them to Him in prayer daily admitting my weakness, so that He could purge me of that.

That justification became a thought pattern that became habitual thought. That habitual thought became obsessive that turned to anger that turned to actions of negativity toward the people I had DECIDED to single out as the "enemy".

No - they were not perfect. Yes, they were negative toward me, too. **But I needed to learn a healthy way to THINK about it, to TALK about it, and to LIVE with it. And that ONLY comes from God.**

* The Blessing that comes with True Realization and Repentance. (In with the NEW!)

What I realized was that God wanted to free me emotionally. He didn't want me to be bitter, and he desired for me to FEEL loved, even when I least expected it. The "rest" that comes with this healing is truly miraculous. As I experienced the release of intentionally NOT speaking, thinking, or allowing myself to feel anger at any of those people, and instead dwell upon the Word of God, I woke up one day to realize I truly no longer felt anger at them. It was no act! I honestly felt peace. Only God can do that.

The peace went as far as to allow me to give my husband a level of trust that I had never done. You see, from the beginning of our relationship, he always filled me in on every bit of communication with his ex. What gradually began to happen was my anger grew as I felt her tone was disrespectful to me, or to my husband, or I felt manipulated, or taken advantage of... the list goes on and on. Ladies, this went on for years - nearly 13, as a matter of fact!

When I finally let go of this coveted sin, I told my husband I really didn't need to hear about the phone conversations or see the letters or emails. I told him if there was something he felt I truly needed to be filled in on, fine, but otherwise, I just felt I should let it go.

What I experienced was a freedom from irritation because even if she was being nice, I realized I had built up such a level of anger toward her that I wasn't seeing her motives as pure any longer. **I needed to take myself out of the equation.**

Read Luke 5:1 - 11

Here, the fishermen were doing the best they could and coming up with nothing! That's exactly what I was doing.

When Jesus simply said, "... let down your nets."

And suddenly the boat almost sunk because of the size of the catch!

That's what Jesus wants to do with us as step moms. He wants us to be blessed beyond measure! But we have to get rid of the coveted sin first. It gets in His way!

Here's what I saw happen:

1) My husband was more peaceful because he didn't have to listen to my irritation.

2) The communication and arguments lessened between my husband and his ex.

3) My step son NOTICED that I was not involved in the arguments and was not getting irritated with his mom, and this caused him to trust me even more, and love me even more! He actually noticed that I was choosing NOT to be involved in any conflict between my husband and his ex wife, and it made a HUGE difference in the way Lucas viewed me.

4) When my in laws expressed their dislike of the way my husband and I handled a situation with Lucas, and I was verbally attacked, I remained calm!!!!! This was very much unlike me! I was the one who would willingly participate in confrontation, and here I was, after years of this behavior - suddenly on the phone telling my mother in law I loved her, even as she was swearing and yelling awful things at me.

   By the same token - I started to tell God I forgave my mother in law, even before she was remorseful - that was obedience to God! Forgiving BEFORE the world wants you to - and in doing so, my mother in law was regretful of her actions within days. What a blessing.

5) I felt a peace - some call it Sabbath Rest - when you go through turmoil, and yet, no matter what the tribulation is - you have peace. No racing of the heart - calmness and peace, and a genuine feeling that things are truly going to be alright. That, my dear friends, is GOD, and God's power alone!

This week I challenge you to ask God what your coveted sin is. Is it justifying your divorce? Is it justifying your husband's divorce, making the ex sound like the worst person on earth? Is it feeling justified at being angry for the treatment you have endured? Is it a leaning on a glass of wine? A habit to smoke a cigarette? Gossip?

Discover what your coveted sin is - we ALL have these strongholds that keep us from a freeing relationship with Christ. If we can truly identify what it is, God will help us overcome that sin, and we will experience a peace like a river.

* Obedience leads to Peace:

Read 2 Chronicles 14:1-6.

2 Chronicles 14: 2 says, "Asa did what was good and right in the eyes of the Lord his God.......verse 6... And the Lord gave him rest."

And then, once we are obedient in confessing coveted sin, and ridding ourselves of it, more peace engulfs us.

In John 14:27, Jesus talked about the kind of peace He brings through the Holy Spirit, "Peace I leave with you; my peace I give you. **I do not give to you as the world gives.** Do not let your hearts be troubled."

Jesus can give us a peace in rough situations that the world cannot give us, and that the world cannot understand. But you, a step mom living in Christ, can have it and experience it, tell others about it, and empower other step mothers to be victorious!

This week, remember God is pruning YOU. You are not changing others, and that is not your job. God is allowing that difficult situation with the ex and with your step children TO CHANGE YOU!! He is improving *your* character. He loves you!

Chapter 4: Your Sounding Board

Who is your sounding board?

When something goes wrong in your life, who do you call immediately?

Who do you like to "dish" with?

It may surprise you to find that almost all of us use the wrong sounding board at some point in our life.

In this lesson, we will identify who we use, why we use them, why we might be using the wrong sounding board, what characteristics we need in a "healthy" sounding board, and how to change sounding boards without alienating someone whom we love dearly but may not be helping us they way God wishes us to be "helped".

We will also touch on why quiet time with God is the best sounding board each of us neglects. And, perhaps hardest of all, we will identify whose sounding board we are, and how we can improve ourselves for them to glorify God!

Who is yours?

Who do you call when something goes wrong in your step mothering?

_____

Most of us choose **someone who will agree with us, not challenge us**.

Think about it. Is your sounding board someone who will tell you that you may have made a mistake in whatever instance you are describing, or are they the one who will immediately agree with whatever you did, or immediately talk about how "tough you have it".

We usually choose someone to be our sounding board who will see things as us being victimized, feel sympathy for our situation, and encourage us, "not to take that!"

This is not done intentionally. This person is probably one of our "safe people". Someone whom we love, and who loves us deeply.

This person is not bad, or wrong. But *we* are wrong to sound off and then leave the moment feeling justified.

For years, my sounding board was my mother. Let me tell you why this was not smart!

My mother is my biggest fan, wholly supportive of me, and she loves me absolutely unconditionally.

But she wants what we all want as mothers for our children.

She wants me to wake up each day, and have no conflict. She hates when there is any problem concerning my step child or my husband's ex. She feels I deserve "better" - a picture perfect June Cleaver life.

I hope we are all mature enough by now to know that TV life doesn't truly exist.

More dangerously, as I was sounding off about whatever dilemma was occurring at the time, I was also encouraging and empowering my mother to feel very negative emotions about my husband, my stepson, and my husband's ex.

As I was "venting", I was causing her pain by causing her to worry about her daughter, and feel I was in a mess.

Then, even as a problem was resolved, there were times when I was too busy or simply forgot to fill her in on the blessings and forgiveness that might have occurred. Soon, a chilliness grew toward my husband and stepson, a feeling that they were "wronging" me on a daily basis.

And this started from my own mouth!

Luke 6:45 For out of the overflow of the heart, the mouth speaks.

Taming our own tongues is the hardest thing we may ever do. It is a daily battle.

Think about your own sounding board:

Now, will this person encourage you to pray immediately - will they see things as "possible" or impossible... will they tell you to be loving, or support you in your anger?

It was a friend of mine who pointed out to me that I was using my mother to reinforce unhealthy thought patterns, and even behavior patterns.

She simply asked me, "Do you know what your mother will say before you speak to her about your latest problem with step mothering? Do you know she is going to agree with whatever you say, and feel sorry for you?"

Stupefied - and feeling stupid - I said, "Of course, she's going to agree with me - she's my mom!"

I love when God uses an unexpected person to get a point across to us, and we are finally forced to shut up and listen!

She said to me, "If your mother isn't encouraging you to love Steve and work it out, it's based on what you have said. Steve loves you. I can see it. Everyone can. You are strong, and you will get through this. Sure, some times are tougher than others, but you are in this for the long haul. Start over tomorrow, don't tell your mom how awful things are. Tell her the GOOD stuff, and see if you feel better."

Can someone say, DUH. She was talking about me CONTROLLING my tongue, not trying to "get people on my side" as we all did in Junior high school.

What I realized immediately is that one of the reasons I have this friend is that whenever she spoke of her "problems", it was with a smile on her face, and a humorous quip at the end of her story. I never left her feeling as though she was overwhelmed.

But I realized that day that I certainly had made my sounding board feel that I was in over my head, and overwhelmed.

Praise God for those moments. That was the moment I stopped focusing on the bad stuff, and followed what God says to do in His word: Philippians 4:8, "Whatever is true, whatever is noble, whatever is right, whatever is pure, whatever is lovely, whatever is admirable - if anything is excellent or praiseworthy - think about such things."

If, when you are sharing things with your sounding board, you feel immediately supported in anger, encouraged to be angry, even encouraged to have that "you don't deserve that" attitude, you are not using a healthy Christian sounding board.

And it's not a great base to build for the next time you see your husband, or your step children, or your husband's ex.

Most of us have had the wrong sounding boards, which is why we turn to therapy at times!

Another friend simply said to me one day, when I was spewing about the unfair treatment I had received, "Do you believe Steve loves you? Because I really think he does."

God can use anyone to figuratively smack us in the face!

Remember that command? LOVE. Oh yeah….. Can I do that after I am finished complaining about how my marriage isn't the way it's "supposed" to be? Absolutely not. We will then face our men with our arms blocking their hugs, we will find ourselves dismissing their attempts at making us feel beautiful and loved. Ladies, our men love us.

Remember that - THEY LOVE US. You'd be surprised at how many step moms have told me they don't feel loved. Yet, as we talk longer, they realize they are loved, and they know they are loved, but ***they have convinced themselves they aren't loved appropriately, or enough.***

And they've done this by relying on the wrong sounding boards, who have let the step moms hurting heart flow freely out of their mouth, instead of fixing the hurt, healing the hurt, focusing on the LOVE that does exist.

I actually saw this happen while I was visiting a step mom friend of mine. She was complaining about how her husband can't pick up the stepson and it's become her job as step mom. (This happens a lot to many of us.) She felt taken advantage of - by her own man, the ex, and even the child.

My friend's husband got home from work, and when he came in and tried to hug her and kiss her, she was at the sink, doing dishes, and didn't look at him. His kiss fell on her cheek, not the lips which were still warm from the negative feelings she had just thrown out of them.

I could see he wanted to embrace her, but she had shut down, feeling like a servant. And I could relate, because I had also felt that both my husband and his ex felt part of my job was to make their "transfers of the child" easier.

We forget that our men want desperately to take care of us, and they are now dealing with failure issues when they realize it's not easy for us to deal with step children and an ex. **As much as we wanted the knight on his white horse, our husbands also WANT to be that to us!!**

Let's look deeper into your sounding board:

1. Name - relationship _____
   _____
   _____

2. How long have they been your sounding board? _____
   _____
   _____

3. What situations have they helped you through - I mean really helped you through - not just listening but actively encouraging and praying and leading??? Don't be surprised if you have to admit, ummmm… none - they are the just the person I use to talk to who I know will validate my feelings of being treated poorly and the great big gasp I enjoy hearing when telling a good story…….

_____
_____
_____
_____
_____
_____

4. What pain has this person been through? Be honest because we need to look at the baggage they are bringing into YOUR relationship and why they might be the wrong person to talk to.

_____
_____
_____

5. Even the disciples had sounding boards - and they were considered the "strong" in faith, right? Why then did they bicker among themselves over who was the greatest??? Luke 9:46-48 says, "An argument started among the disciples as to which of them would be the greatest. Jesus, knowing their thoughts, took a little child and had him stand beside him. Then he said to them, "Whoever welcomes this little child in my name welcomes me; and whoever welcomes me welcomes the one who sent me. For he who is least among you all - he is the greatest."

6. Write a prayer to God, ask Him to give you the proper sounding board?

_____
_____

7. When did you turn to Him first?
   For some reason, we forget God wants us to speak to Him. Tell Him your feelings, your insecurities, pray He will help you, and He will. Don't limit the power He has and what He can do for you.

_____
_____
_____

8. Write down what you think the "proper" sounding board would be and say, when hearing your complaints.

_____
_____
_____
_____

9. Now write down what you think Christ would say about your current sounding board.

_____

_____

_____

_____

10. Who do you think God would want you to sound off to now?

_____

_____

_____

This doesn't mean you cut ties to your current sounding board - **it means you stop the behavior that YOU are adding to the unhealthy part of this sounding board relationship**.

When you want to "sound off", pray instead. When you want to share positives, then share. Take control of your tongue - the hardest thing for any of us to tame.

Be honest with your sounding board, that you need positive encouragement - tell them, "I need to talk about this, but I want to begin by telling you that although I am angry, I need to be encouraged NOT to leave my husband, but to forgive him and love him. Can you help me be more positive in my thinking?"

To God, sounding off in a negative fashion is the same as gossiping.

Let's remind ourselves where God stands on gossip.

Exodus 23:1 Do not spread false reports. Do not help a wicked man by being a malicious witness.

We might be telling the truth - *but it's the truth from our perspective*. If we are criticizing the way our husband handled a situation, that's gossip. **We are making our sounding board our "malicious witness"** *by changing the way they view the people we talk about!!*

Proverbs 25:18 Like a club or a sword or a sharp arrow is the man who gives false testimony against his neighbor.

Be the one who is lied about, not the one talking about how awful the ex is, or the step children. **Be honorable!!**

2 Thessalonians 3:11-12 We hear that some among you are idle. They are not busy; they are busybodies. Such people we command and urge in the Lord Jesus Christ to settle down and earn the bread they eat.

Choose not to talk about the ex, or the step children, or the in laws, or your husband - in a negative way. Yes, it goes back to, "If you can't say something nice, don't say anything at all." This is hard!! We want to be encouraged and appreciated, and if we feel we are not, then we will seek it out! This is why we need to DAILY be in the Word for encouragement. I have had days when I have read the entire book of Psalm, and when I was finished, every time, I felt refreshed and encouraged! I KNEW God was looking out for me.

One stumbling block I had to face was when my mother in law became the sounding board for my husband's ex. This gave them a chance to "sound off" about me, about what they didn't like, what they didn't approve of, etc. Many step moms have this happen.

It was hard to admit that I didn't like it, but the real reason I truly didn't like it was because for years, <u>I had been doing the same thing</u>! I had certainly said negative things to my mother in law about my husband's ex. This was a "dose of my own medicine".

And it was a lesson from God!! He wanted me to see this unhealthy situation from both sides, and understand how much it hurt people.

After 11 years, I finally learned that if my mother in law and the ex needed to sound off to each other about me, that I determined I would rather be the one talked about and NOT the one talking about people.

You see, God doesn't put these people who, to us, seem "difficult" in our lives for US to change. He puts them there to CHANGE US, to improve our character and our honor, and to make us grow *in how maturely we react to them*.

If we only learn how to deal with easy people, how does that make us a better person to be used for Christ? It doesn't.

Only when we deal with the hard people in our lives and deal with them the way Christ would - that's when we are a blessing to God!!

You can do this, ladies. Trust God.

PEACE. God's peace covered me the moment I realized I needed to stop talking about what I perceived to be "wrong" about certain people.

Focus on the good, don't obsess over the bad.

Psalm 57:4 says

I am in the midst of lions; I lie among ravenous beasts - men whose teeth are spears and arrows, whose tongue are sharp swords.

We feel like that, don't we? Everyone does in some situation some time. Don't pick up a chair to go head to head with those lions. Let God. Give it to God, and be still. Give it to Him.

Now, let's turn the tables.

Whose sounding board are you?

What was the last thing you told this person? Was it something that pointed them back to Christ or back to self absorbed whining?

_____
_____
_____
_____

Do you think you have encouraged this person to get into the Word? Have you reminded this person of positives?

_____
_____
_____
_____
_____

What I realized is that I had become the sounding board of a step mother in a bible study I was attending. As I listened to her stories, I would nod, and reinforce her feelings of being treated badly by her step kids, the ex, the in laws, and her husband. But I realized after far too many get-togethers, that I wasn't building her up in Christ. I had successfully empowered her into realizing that most of us step moms go through these times, but I hadn't given her anything firm to hold onto that was good, and life building.

I needed to remind her that her husband loves her, that Christ loves her, and that she is going to be victorious!

Speak <u>LIFE</u> into the person using you as their sounding board. Give them a verse of scripture that will help them focus on God and his word, rather than whatever attack they are facing that day.

One of my favorites is Isaiah 35: 3-4:

Strengthen the feeble hands, steady the knees that give way; say to those with fearful hearts, "Be strong, do not fear; your God will come, he will come with vengeance; with divine retribution he will come to save you."

God's saving grace did not separate the alliance between my husband's ex and my mother in law, nor did He choose to stop their words about me.

He was much mightier than that!

He granted me peace. He took away the part of me that clamored for the approval of my mother in law, and the anger I had that the ex was saying negative things about me.

He showed me first hand how much it hurts when someone gossips about you, and in doing so, it stopped my mouth in saying things about my mother in law and the ex.

God changed me, my thinking, my heart. He showed me to FOCUS on the good, His grace, His LOVE, and not to obsess on the bad - the gossips, the lies, the verbal attacks.

Suddenly, there was that Sabbath rest again. Wow - does Satan hate that!!!!

He orchestrates these cruel attacks that would have leveled me just a few months ago, but since I have chosen obedience to God, God has thwarted those attacks, and taught me to "Be still and KNOW that I am God."

I can't tell you how many times I read that scripture, but to LIVE it, and to FEEL it is something I cannot put into words.

I was a people pleaser - I wanted the ex to approve of me, and like me. I wanted my in laws to embrace me. I wanted my stepson to think I walked on water, figuratively speaking, of course.

When I realized that I was in control of what I did to please people, I saw how ridiculous it was!

God created us for HIS purpose. When I finally - at age 38 - gave him ME, full submission, he gave me peace in midst of a storm - calmness in the presence of lions.

That is not in me, ladies. Not at all. That is Christ in me, leading me as I finally gave up my control.

Let Him take you by the hand this week, as you relinquish your control, and identify your sounding board.

This is exciting - He loves you SO MUCH!!!!

Points to Ponder this week:

Focus V. Obsession

This week I want you to try to identify what has become an obsession to you, and what God would say you should truly need to be focusing on.

I had to realize the conflicts were becoming obsessive. They were so irritating to me - the legal battles, the arguments, etc. - that I was actually dwelling on them. This happens to most people in hard times. Unfortunately, as step moms, we sometimes have these times more frequently. An argument between our husband and his ex may involve us, or may just upset us. The step child might get involved and get mad at your husband, or you, and then the one conflict becomes two. And then you and your husband may argue over it, and suddenly it's three conflicts. And then if your in laws have an opinion, it's four. And that can be just one day.....

What do we do with all that? No, we don't run screaming down the street.... Although we do think about it... ha ha.

We get back to Philippians 4:8, "Whatever is true, whatever is noble, whatever is right, whatever is pure, whatever is lovely, whatever is admirable - if anything is excellent or praise-worthy - think about such things."

Wow, this is one of the hardest things to master, isn't it?? What I learned is I needed to sometimes take myself out of the equation so that I was focusing on the good, and not obsessing over the bad.

There was a time when the ex would request to speak to me instead of Steve, feeling that I "listened and understood" better. Do not do this. Ever. This is an affront on your union with your husband. If you take that seat for him, you are 1)taking away part of what God determines to be the head of your household, and 2) allowing someone to make you feel you are better at handling things than your man. This is the Deceiver planting little seeds of aggravation and doubt. Eventually, the ex and I would have a conflict, and then the cycle continued. This went on for years. Until last year when I truly felt God was telling me to actively submit to Steve. Steve had not requested it. I felt God wanted me to cut involvement for my own sake. I never said, "I'm not talking to you anymore!" I simply told Steve I really felt he needed to handle these things and that he and his ex needed to decide things about their child together.

When there are conflicts, if you don't obsess about them, and think about them all day, then this is great! You are focusing on godly and good things about your family and your husband!

If you, like me, find yourself irritated and going over it in your mind, get in the Word so God will FOCUS you and take away the Deceiver's obsessive attacks.

Controlling your thoughts

Micah 2:1-2 says "Woe to those who plan iniquity, to those who plot evil on their beds! At morning's light they carry it out because it is in their power to do it. They covet fields and seize them, and houses, and take them. They defraud a man of his home, a fellowman of his inheritance."

My Life Application Bible describes this scripture as .... **A person's thoughts and plans reflect his or her character.** What do you think about as you lie down to sleep? Do your desires involve greed or stepping on others to achieve your goals? Evil thoughts lead to evil deeds."

Titus 1:15 To the pure, all things are pure, but to those who are corrupted and do not believe, nothing is pure. In fact, both their minds and consciences are corrupted.

We want to be pure in the eyes of God. *But if we are irritated with the way our step children spoke to us, or how the ex spoke to us, we are allowing our thoughts to become more important than our relationship with Christ.* If we then allow it to evolve into behavior, our character has been diminished from what it should be.

My stepson was rude to me, so I intentionally slept in when he was leaving for school the next day. When I tried to do my quiet time, I felt guilty. Even if I feel wronged, I choose to sin if I try to seek revenge, even simple revenge like choosing not to do something I'd done for 6 years. Even when no apology came, I needed to obey God, forgive with no apology thereby CONTROLLING my thoughts, and conquering Satan once again. I got up the next morning, made him breakfast, put out the Bible verse of the day, laid out the prayer journal for him to add his prayer requests and praises, and set his lunch on the table.

Why was I surprised that when he came down, and saw that, that he immediately apologized for his fresh mouth? God is good. He touches hearts when we obey Him and do what He wants us to do, even when it's a struggle to do so.

Control your thoughts, and that leads to you controlling your actions for God's glory.

Changing your attitude:

I'm copying a paragraph from my Life Application Bible for this lesson because it is a wonderful warning on how our attitudes can lead us down an alley we don't want to go down.

Numbers 16:41 "The next day the whole Israelite community grumbled against Moses and Aaron. "You have killed the Lord's people," they said.

Page 244 in the Life Application Bible says of this verse, "Just one day after Korah and his followers were executed for grumbling and complaining against God, the Israelites started all over with more muttering and complaining. Their negative attitude only caused them to rebel even more and to bring about even greater trouble. It eroded their faith in God and encouraged thoughts of giving up and turning back. The path to open rebellion against God begins with dissatisfaction and skepticism, then moves to grumbling about both God and present circumstances. Next comes bitterness and resentment, followed finally by rebellion and open hostility. If you are often dissatisfied, skeptical, complaining or bitter - beware! These attitudes lead to rebellion and separation from God. Any choice to side against God is a step in the direction of letting go of him completely and making your own way through life."

Does that speak to us as step mothers, or what??? It sneaks up on us - that feeling of dissatisfaction - maybe it started from feeling taken advantage of - feeling isolated… suddenly, without our awareness, it grew into this "thing" that causes us negative feelings, bitterness, etc.

And then those actions come up… here's one of my biggest failures:

I was feeling quite attacked by my step son and the ex. I felt they were badgering my husband with all these negative views of me and that my husband was believing them. (It took me years to realize the views were truly not deterring my husband's feelings for me - but my perception was erred, and I had convinced myself my husband was turning against me in favor of the step son and the ex and their views of circumstances. This is something many step moms start to believe.)

I wrote a fake email, and left it out for my step son to see. It made it sound as though he was a real problem and he should appreciate me for all I do, etc. Just plain stupid, and just plain sinful. I placed it somewhere I knew he would see it. My flesh wanted to hurt him the way I felt he and the ex had hurt me. I was feeling vengeful because I felt wronged. When I knew he had seen it, I then threw it away, and lied about it when he told my husband about seeing it.

It was two days of lying about it before I finally came clean. I actually started therapy after that because - thank God - I realized that I felt so bitter over feeling the ex "expected" me to do everything she wasn't doing for her son, and I felt resentment over my step son not waving a banner in front of my face thanking me daily, AND I had convinced myself my husband wasn't in my corner. That moved me to grumbling, as the scripture describes above, and finally open hostility which came about when I sinned by trying to hurt my stepson with a fake letter, and then lying about it.

It took me years to regain my stepson's trust. That was a consequence to my sin. Yes, God forgave me when I was finally remorseful after two days (shame on me!), but I still had to face the consequences. Yes, Lucas forgave me, but my consequence was building back his trust in me.

Have you done something deliberately to hurt your step children, to "get back at them" for treatment you perceive is wrong? Or the ex?

Confess it to God, to yourself, to the one wronged. Purge yourself of this sin, even if it is hidden. Clean out the junk.

I went through therapy because I truly thought I was losing it! I couldn't believe I had done such a thing. I learned it was all about the feelings, the thoughts, the attitudes, the bitterness, the resentment…. Whoa - that finally turned to action… ugly action.

We are not perfect. I prayed my wrong was an example to Lucas that we all mess up big, but we can make up for our actions, confess them, and try again. Don't try to be the perfect step mom, mom or wife. Be what God wants you to be. Forgiven. Loved. Loving. Forgiving.

Romans 8:28 And we know that in all things God works for the good of those who love him, who have been called according to his purpose.

God can turn everything around for his glory. I saw this in Lucas, when he made some teenage mistakes, that included lying about me to some people. I forgave him…. That second. Again, that is not me! That is Christ in me. I never would have believed when I lied for two days about that foolish email that the forgiveness that was coming so hard for Lucas during that time would be turned around to teach him a lesson in forgiveness. When he messed up, he knew me forgiving him immediately was a sacrifice because he had been on the other end! Isn't God amazing? He took my sin - the sin the Devil rejoiced over for about a minute - and he turned it into a lesson for Lucas, and for me.

Lucas knew how badly he wanted that forgiveness from me, and he realized - two years after my sin against him - how I had felt when I so badly wanted his forgiveness.

God had allowed all of it so that Lucas and I would both learn the freeing power of forgiveness. We had both learned how ugly sin is, and we had both learned how much people who love us truly want forgiveness for their sins. That was Romans 8:28 in action, in LIFE!!

This WILL happen in your lives. God wants everything to be turned around for HIS GLORY!

Chapter 5: Momming and Out-momming

No, it's not a "real" word. I define "Outmomming" as when the biological mother feels you, as the step mom, are trying to "out mom" her, outdo her in her role as a mother.

This is extremely common, and I have yet to meet a step mother who hasn't been accused of this.

One summer, I wrote Ann and asked her if she could buy my stepson track shoes before she brought him back from his visit with her. He would need the shoes the very day he returned. She agreed in a nice email back to me, but then told my stepson, "I don't need a step mom telling me when my son needs shoes!"

She felt I was Outmomming her. She felt I was telling her something she wouldn't know to do.

Most of this is just a feeling, but it's important to recognize what sometimes develops behind these feelings.

Proverbs 21:2 says "All a man's ways seem right to him, but the Lord weighs his heart."

We need to examine our motives. I can honestly say my motives were not negative in asking Ann to buy those shoes. But there was also another time in which Lucas returned back from a visit carrying a pink suitcase. I indignantly bought him another that I determined was more "boy like" and shipped the pink one back. My motives were clearly negative and critical in doing so.

I needed to follow biblical teaching, not try to "one up" her with a suitcase. Matthew 6:3-4 says, "When you give to the needy, do not let your left hand know what your right hand is doing, so that your giving may be in secret. Then your Father, who sees what is done in secret, will reward you."

I needed to do things for Lucas without her seeing it. I needed to do for Lucas, and do it FOR him. In this way, I was pleasing God, not man.

I needed to change my thinking of doing anything for Lucas just because Ann wasn't doing it. That was causing resentment within me.

What starts happening to most step moms is that every time they do what they think the "mom" should be doing, they unconsciously start keeping a mental list of her shortcomings, and a *very* long list of their "doings" for their stepchildren.

Step moms Brittany and Tina lived this scripture in Matthew in their dealings with the ex and with their step children.

The ex bought Alyssa new socks, and Brittany made a point to thank her for doing that. And she thanked her in front of Alyssa. This encouraged the good behavior of simply buying socks. It showed gratitude and grace from the step mom to the mom. And it showed maturity in relationships to little Alyssa. That's what the Matthew scripture is all about.

When Whitney needed a new dress for a father-daughter event, the ex wanted the father, Tina's husband, to go shopping and get it. Instead, step mom Tina offered to take the step daughter and buy the dress. This was an example to Whitney that her activities and what she wanted to do was important to Tina. This encouraged Whitney to be appreciative, and express that sort of behavior to Tina. It also showed the ex that Tina was available for her daughter. That is the Matthew scripture in action.

When Lucas visited us, and Ann had custody, she was in charge of doctor's visits, dental appointments, sporting events, etc. Those are normally the "mom" duties. She did the running around, and the picking up here and there.

But, nowadays, more step moms than ever before are becoming the "mom" when their husbands gain custody of the children. When this happens, things change dramatically, and neither household seems to know what to expect, or how anyone will react.

There was no custody fight when Lucas came to live with us. He was rebellious and lacking discipline, and Ann was inconsistent with discipline. (That is not a criticism - it is very common for divorced parents to be too easy on discipline and not follow through - more on that in the next lesson.) Lucas came to us at age 12, when Steve and I had just had our first little girl, Grace.

I truly think Ann simply thought Steve would completely rearrange his work schedule to handle doctor and dentist appointments, and the like. It was quite bothersome to her that I was choosing Lucas' doctors and dentists, and then taking him to his appointments, and making medical decisions regarding his health.

I thought she would want to be involved in what was happening, since she lived in Iowa, and we lived in Arizona, so after each visit, I would email her with the diagnosis, etc. I thought I was doing what I would want to know as a mom. But, what it was doing to her was reminding her that SHE wasn't doing it. Sure, she wanted to know, just not from another woman who was raising her son. My mother in law told me several times, "You're his mom now."

That is the view most women have, with so many mothers sending their children go to live with their fathers.

And then there's the social stigma of a woman who doesn't have custody of her own children.

Let's face it, women can be harsh on other women, can't they? If a woman doesn't have custody of her children, the immediate assumption is, "BAD MOM". It's not right, but it's what a lot of people seem to feel.

While in our custody, Lucas had three surgeries - he had his tonsils out, a small tumor removed from his leg, and he had his wisdom teeth removed. In all of those instances, I was the one who got him to and from all of the doctor appointments, and I was the only one of all "four" parents who was present for all the surgeries. Ann came to one, and my husband came to only two. The step dad did not attend any. The point I am trying to make is not "hooray for me!" - the point I am trying to make is - what was the message to Lucas?

The message to Lucas was: "My dad is too busy working. My mom is too involved with her life in another state with her husband and adopted baby."

Lucas began saying to everyone, "I feel like I am not being raised by my mom OR my dad. I feel like I'm being raised by my step mom."

And that's exactly what *was* happening. I was a stay at home mom, available when he needed me. And he needed me!

Before coming home full time with Lucas and baby Grace, I was very career oriented as a television reporter.

When I came home, my focus changed entirely. I loved the mom duties, and embraced them, as I had my career.

Lucas was very involved in sports, and so in his 7th grade, I loaded Grace up in the carrier or the stroller, and off we went to baseball games, football games, band concerts… everything.

And here's where the world perception again attacks the ex, and benefits us in a very strange way.

If a dad is absent, no one looks at the step dad, and says, "Wow, what a great guy for being here."

But, for some odd reason, when a step mom attends all of her stepchildren's events, we are seen as martyrs. The fact that the mom wasn't at a band concert in Arizona when she lived in Iowa didn't matter. Other moms saw this as "bad", and therefore, the step moms - us, as "good".

Steve and I got pregnant with our second little girl, Lulu Bay, and moved to Indiana.

Lucas' 8th grade was tough! I strapped one baby on with the Bjorn carrier, and put the other one in the stroller, and went to all his track meets and baseball and football games.

It was hard, but Lucas recognized I was doing it so he would have someone there. And I truly believe that's what God wanted me to do.

Ann lived in Iowa and my husband worked long hours, and as we all know, sometimes these school events are at 3, 4, and 5 o'clock so it's hard for working parents to make it.

I also came to realize what God was doing *for me*. He was getting me up and getting me out! With two babies, it would have been very easy for me to want to stay home all day and just love on them. But Lucas needed me, too. And every time - **every single time** - Lucas would say to me, "Thanks for coming."

That was a blessing. God was letting me feel appreciated, and urging Lucas to tell me so. And when we are encouraged, we want to do even more!

In Lucas' senior year, I had a mom say to me, "I remember you in the kids 8th grade - with those two babies! I can't believe you came to all that!"

God knows our motives. Lucas needed a parent there. I was simply the only one available. And it mattered! We all know kids who have their parents together, and still their parents don't show up to things the kids are involved in. And we know how it makes those kids feel when after the games, there's no one to say, "great job".

Lucas' mother was never able to be a stay at home mom due to finances, and because of that, she was not able to simply fly or drive to see his events. She came in for one football game a year, and tried to come for one baseball game a year, if possible. Remember, she had to work. But, still, the stigma was there - the other parents saw me at everything. Most assumed I was Lucas' mother. So when she came in for a visit, imagine how uncomfortable she was, wearing a shirt with his name on the back and cheering, with all the moms looking and whispering. Ouch.

That was also how she felt I was Outmomming her. I knew all the other mothers. I was involved in the volunteer organizations. I was doing everything she had to give up when she lived out of state.

As I said, when you are encouraged, you only want to do more. And that's what I did.

In Lucas' senior year, I was elected as vice president of the parents association for his football team. This was such a blessing because I had gotten to know so many moms, and loved the women who were involved. I loved the chit chat about who was doing what, and what kids we needed to watch out for - we need to be careful FOR ALL our children and the temptations out there.

I did it because Lucas loved that I was involved. It made him feel important that he had a family member doing things for the team.

That same year, the ex moved to town, 5 miles away from us.

I invited her to be a part of everything - selling clothes to make money for the football team, making breakfast for the senior players on game days, making food for the team before the sectional playoffs, etc. She chose to do none of it.

And why would she? We need to be compassionate and understand what it's like to be on that side!!

When we had visitation, and Steve and I would visit Lucas in Iowa, the other moms were quite nice to me. Why? Because I was "just" the mom's ex husband's wife to them. ***I wasn't in the "mom territory" or breaking any boundaries.***

But when the ex moved to town, after 6 years of me being so involved in whatever I could volunteer in, WOW….. I actually had some moms say to me, "This is *your* place. She needs to find something else to do. Where has she been for the last 6 years of his life?!"

Most moms were shocked that I was asking her to be involved. Many would say, "Where's she been? You're the step mom and you're doing all this???"

It was pretty eye opening. And a good lesson on the clear difference between godly views and worldly views. And sometimes those comments can make us stray from the views we have in place from God. There were definitely times when I caught myself thinking the same way - "I'm the step mom and I'm having three breakfasts??? And she's holding none???" That's a worldly view, not godly.

I had to re-focus and set my motives clear again with God. "Lord, please help me not be bitter. Help me want to do this for Your glory, not the world's."

Then, one sectional dinner night, after a week of conflict with the ex, another God incident happened.

The dinner started at 5 pm, and I was surprised the ex had finally volunteered this time to bring a dish. I was feeling pretty angry at her over the most recent conflict, and it took all my strength to not share that with all the women I knew would agree with me! But, thank the Lord, I held my tongue.

5:15 - The football parent's club president's wife asked me, "Do you think she's going to come, Dawn? I'm counting on her casserole."

Bite your tongue….. I said, "Yes, you can count on her. She'll be here." 5:30, 5:45, 6:00. No show.

6:15 - More than an hour late - the dinner over, the players leaving, the ex comes in the front door of the school.

ALL the moms turn around. We are all cleaning up. The whispering begins. "Who is that?", "Doesn't she know it was more than a hour ago?"

Lucas runs up to her, and ushers her out quickly. I can see that she is mortified and desperately embarrassed.

And I immediately feel sorry for her!

My anger toward her was washed away in an instant! You see, God knows our hearts and our motives better than we do. He knew the ex was lashing out at me that week. And He knew I was feeling angry.

I believe he allowed this to happen to show me compassion for my "enemy".

I sincerely and truly felt sorry for her!! Only God can change our hearts in an instant like that.

Luke 18:11-14 says "The Pharisee stood up and prayed about himself: 'God, I thank you that I am not like other men - robbers, evildoers, adulterers - or even like this tax collector. I fast twice a week and give a tenth of all I get.' But the tax collector stood at a distance. He would not even look up to Heaven, but beat his breast and said, 'God, have mercy on me, a sinner.'

Jesus said, "I tell you that this man, rather than the other, went home justified before God. For everyone who exalts himself will be humbled, and he who humbles himself will be exalted."

We need to make sure our motives are right, and our attitudes, and our actions.

I regretted being prideful about my anger toward the ex in the INSTANT I saw the way the world and the other moms reacted to her making a simple mistake of showing up late. That is godly compassion. Praise God whenever he reveals something like this to you! **He is changing your character, and improving you for His glory.**

KNOW YOUR ROLE:

We step moms also need to know when to back off, and let the moms "mom".

When the ex moved here in May, Lucas' baseball season was in full swing.

Every other year, I had gone to all the games. This year, I made a difficult decision to attend only the home games. I felt God urging me that sometimes Lucas needed to have his mom there, and not feel torn at the end of the game. I also felt she needed to get that mom spotlight to herself sometimes.

Especially when there's conflict, it's our job to bow out gracefully. Don't make this a message of martyrdom. Don't point out that you are doing this.

Just do it.

If you need an excuse, sign up for a class that meets at that time, or sign your kids up for an activity. Do something that will allow the stepchild to have his parents together once in a while. They need this. They love their mom and dad. They love you.

They need to have them together - if only for a moment after a game or event - to BOTH encourage them.

It's 10 minutes. Give it to them.

I truly believe that sometimes the step children just need the step parents to lie low once in a while.

She's not taking your place in the eyes of the stepchildren. They won't forget what you've done for them, and how much you've attended, and what you've done, etc.

Going a step further, I asked Ann to take over the baseball stuff since I was the football mom - she worked two concession stands and she appreciated it VERY much!

That was how I backed off a little and made sure she felt I was letting her "mom" and not Outmomming her. No, it wasn't easy. ***But sometimes giving that "glory" away is exactly what God wants you to do.*** God sees it.

Luke 14:1 "For everyone who exalts himself will be humbled, and he who humbles himself will be exalted."

We've covered a lot of introspective things so far, cleaning out our thinking, refocusing our hearts and minds. Next lesson we being to empower ourselves! Step motherhood is not just about improving your character. It is also about claiming what is rightfully yours in a loving and definitive way.

Next we talk about YOUR MAN, YOUR HOUSE, and YOUR FAMILY. Not hers. YOURS.

Chapter 6: EMPOWERMENT SECTION!

Your MAN, Your MARRIAGE, Your FAMILY

It's fairly common for a step mom or a step dad to feel they are in someone else's place, at times. Sometimes our lives become so set on the most recent conflict with the ex or the stepchild, or our husband, that we don't realize we are looking at ourselves as "the woman raising someone else's children". When what we need to remember is this is OUR place.

Your MAN:

I remember a time my stepson was angry with his stepfather. Lucas had been mouthy and disrespectful to his mother, and the stepfather had finally intervened and told Lucas, "Don't speak to my wife like that!" Lucas was angry, but the stepfather was entirely correct.

We marry someone with a goal of spending our lives with them. We don't have children with the same goal. We are responsible to God to bring up the child according to God's biblical teachings, but we are to "train up a child in the way he should go and when he is old, he will not depart from it." (Proverbs 22:6) **We let go, and we let God.**

What I've seen and what I've heard from other step mothers is that the line is blurred with children of divorce and their parents. They feel rejected from one or both of the parents who divorced, and they unconsciously are trying to reinforce to themselves that they are "number one" in the parents' lives. They make the parent(s) feel guilty, they act out, and deep down, most feel unloved in some respect.

Lucas was staking a claim on his mother by being rude to her in front of the step dad - challenging him to a duel. The line was blurred as to who was the parent and who was the child.

Ann is a mother, but first she is a wife. The stepfather will spend his life with Ann. Lucas won't. Lucas will go on and find a life of his own. Some divorced parents forget this. And this causes great conflict in the marital relationship. Suddenly, the child is the "partner", which is supposed to be the place of the spouse.

Lucas also demonstrated this behavior to Steve and me, and successfully interfered in our marital relationship. Little lies here and there, and exaggerations, planted seeds of anger within Steve toward me.

When children do this who are not step children, most parents recognize this and deal with it - but with step children, the behavior can be devastating.

This was completely an unconscious plan on Lucas' part, and one that is mirrored by many children of divorce.

One of my friends, Brian, was raised by his mom who was on her third marriage when I met him. What he realized - and not until he was in his 30s - was that he had so much anger toward his mother that he would constantly plant little seeds of doubt in her mind against her husband(s). Soon her irritation and doubt in her husband(s) were so high that she left again... This happened because Brian's mother was listening to Brian, a child, and taking what he said with the weight she should have given her spouse's opinions. But to his mother, Brian had become the "adult" even though he was barely a teen. His mother would hold everything inside, not realizing resentment for her spouse was building. Then, she would respond to her spouse in a manner that was harsher than she would have - had she not listened to Brian's lies.

In his adult years, Brian came to realize he blamed himself for splitting up his half sisters and half brothers parents, and he realized how selfish and destructive his behavior was to his mother's marriages.

Lucas was/is also angry inside that his parents are divorced. He is angry that his mother and step dad had adopted a baby and in his mind "no longer needed him". (This was actually a phrase he used often to Steve and me! How sad.) And he felt out of place with Steve and I having children together, and watching both households work through conflicts. He couldn't admit it, but it made him angry that his parents "other" children would not be displaced as he was. It made him question how important he was to both his mother and father. He was torn inside, questioning how both of his parents were willing to work through conflicts with their "new" spouses, but were unwilling to work through conflicts together to allow him to have a "normal" household with both of his parents together.

Steve and I went through our first round of marriage counseling with Pastor Eugene Heiskell, of Goodyear First Assembly of God, in Arizona. We learned we had to stop allowing Lucas to plant these seeds within Steve's mind and heart. Steve thought he was being a good father by listening to Lucas' opinions, but ***what we learned was that Steve was NOT being a father, but a friend. Lucas had no clear boundaries with either of his parents*** because they both allowed this.

His mother allowed Lucas to say awful things about her husband, and us, and Steve had also allowed Lucas to say awful things about me, and about his mother and step dad. What they had both done is placed Lucas in an "adult" position. Lucas had erroneously learned that his opinions were more valuable than any adult involved in his life, and he felt very much in control since he realized his manipulation could get him what he wanted in both households.

The step dad told us a story about how he was talking to Lucas one day, telling him again that he was being disrespectful. When Ann came around the corner, the step dad says Lucas recoiled, acting as though he was about to be hit (which he wasn't). Ann flew around the corner, yelled at the step dad, took Lucas in the car and left the house for the entire afternoon.

Lucas won! The marital relationship was damaged. No trust between Ann and her husband, because, in this instance, she had given that to Lucas instead. The step dad says it took two weeks for Ann to realize the truth in what Lucas had done. But by that time, Lucas was empowered and the step dad was hurt. Ann considered what she was doing was protecting her son, but what she had actually done was teach Lucas he was more important than her husband. Lucas was empowered to lie, and to disrespect his step father. *Even when the lie was revealed, Lucas was not expected to apologize to his step dad*. The entire thing was ignored, which again empowered Lucas to have a lofty opinion of himself, higher than his step father's position in his own home. The same thing happened over and over in our house, until we finally got marriage counseling. This is a pattern many step parents live with, afraid to rock the boat in their own homes with their own spouses.

At out counselor's suggestion, Steve and I confronted Lucas about this behavior. He was 12 at the time. To our surprise, he admitted that he knew he was doing this, and that he realized now that he had also attempted to sabotage his mother's marriage. We reassured him we loved him but that the behavior had to stop. In a loving manner, Steve told Lucas, "Dawn and I are not going to get divorced. You need to understand that. We love each other, and this is our family. You are a part of it, but you have to stop trying to demean her."

This was demonstrating unity to Lucas. Our marriage bond - our love.

This boundary also needed to be enforced with the ex. The line was often blurred with her, as well, regarding what was an emotional intimacy.

In the beginning of our relationship, I noticed the ex would speak to Lucas on the phone and then ask to speak with Steve, and at that point, things about her work and her problems with her marriage, etc, were being discussed. In marriage counseling, we learned this was an affront to our unity as a married couple. Discussions about the children, transfers, travel, school and issues are appropriate, however, anything further crosses the marriage boundary. The ex had a husband and needed to lean on him. She was chipping away at her marriage, and at ours, by blurring the line between ex-husband and real husband.

And this is common! I've spoken to so many step moms who see this behavior. Sometimes it's just hard for people to accept divorce even years later. They have a bond with someone they created a life with, and it's hard to ignore it. The answer is not to be mean, just lovingly correct, as the bible dictates.

Steve told her nicely and directly that she needed to share things with her husband, Gunnar, and not Steve.

This is not a jealousy issue at all, ladies. This is YOUR husband. Most step moms were *NOT* the reason their husband's first marriage failed, and most didn't marry their men because, "This will really show her!" No, you married your man because you LOVE him. Making that covenant is nothing small. You made a covenant before God, as did your husband, and you both need to honor that. That means emotional intimacies - sharing stories and feelings - those are meant for the marital union ONLY. Be territorial on this!

Ephesians 5:21 - 33 talks about how our husbands are to love us as Christ loved the church. Christ would not have given that love lightly, and our husbands need to be territorial, too, with who they share emotional stories and feelings to - it should only be *us.*

Ephesians 5:21-33

"Wives, submit to your husbands as to the Lord. For the husband is the head of the wife as Christ is the head of the church, his body, of which he is the Savior. Now as the church submits to Christ, so also wives should submit to their husbands in everything.

Husbands, love your wives, just as Christ loved the church and gave himself up for her to make her holy, cleansing her by the washing with water through the word, and to present her to himself as a radiant church, without stain or wrinkle or any other blemish, but holy and blameless.

In this same way, husbands ought to love their wives as their own bodies. He who loves his wife loves himself. After all, no one ever hated his own body, but he feeds and cares for it, just as Christ does the church— for we are members of his body. "For this reason a man will leave his father and mother and be united to his wife, and the two will become one flesh. "This is a profound mystery—but I am talking about Christ and the church. However, each one of you also must love his wife as he loves himself, and the wife must respect her husband."

Many step moms give up when things get hard. Do not ignore God's word when this happens. ***Your husband is YOUR man.*** I remember one time I was feeling particularly weak, and crying in my bathroom. I was praying that God would urge my husband to come and hold me and comfort me. (He was upset with my stepson and my husband needs to 'cool down" before he can offer physical comfort. This is something I had to learn!)

As I prayed, I felt God tell me, "You don't need any human to hold you. I AM CARRYING YOU." At once, I saw myself being carried by Christ. I was wearing a white robe, as he is so often depicted as wearing. I was leaning my head on his shoulder, and I realized I felt complete peace and protection. No fear. It was so childlike, as a father carrying his little girl. At once, I felt the wondrous goose bumps of the Holy Spirit, the comforter. Within 20 minutes, Steve came to me. I was reading Psalms. He knelt in front of me, and just held me, saying over and over, "I love you…"

Steve is my man, and GOD IS IN CONTROL. ***When we lean on Him, he will move people to do things that are a blessing to us.*** I am so thankful Christ loves me. And he wants to comfort you, too.

Your MARRIAGE.

Malachi 2:14, 15 says "You ask, "Why?" It is because the Lord is acting as the witness between you and your wife, because you have broken faith with her, though she is your partner, the wife of your covenant. Has not the Lord made them one? In flesh and spirit they are his. And why one? Because he was seeking godly offspring. So guard yourself in your spirit, and do not break faith with your wife."

This passage is so awesome to step moms! Breaking faith with your wife doesn't just mean adultery. It means allowing anyone else to be in that emotional intimacy circle - it could be the ex, the stepchildren, the in laws… It could even be our own minds convincing us of something that isn't accurate!

Marriage counseling is such a wonderful thing that God has allowed people to master in order to save marriages and help people. Rick Sudsberry, a counselor in Avon, IN, was absolutely a godsend to Steve and me. During a particularly hard time in our marriage, we turned again to counseling. Sudsberry is a Christian with an Assemblies of God University education.

At the time, Lucas was in trouble with drugs, and the ex was telling Steve that I was too hard on Lucas, and my husband was questioning whether I was. Sudsberry helped us realize that what was happening was that I was feeling isolated, with a complete lack of support. The ex was out of state, and Steve traveled quite a bit. I was trying to enforce discipline and help guide Lucas back to the right path, and yet, I felt these two parents were completely unsupportive of me. Those seeds of doubt the ex had planted had sprouted into a vine choking Steve's faith in me, and causing resentment and anger within me. I was figuratively standing on a soap box, yelling, "*I am trying to get this kid back on track and all you two can do is criticize me*?!"

In my quiet time, I felt God say, "Dawn, you don't need to defend yourself. I AM YOUR DEFENDER."

In the very next session, Steve sat there, crying, telling Sudsberry how much he realized I did for Lucas and that I was truly trying to make sure he was a good kid, and how he realized I felt unappreciated. Sudsberry told Steve not to allow Lucas, or the ex, or Steve's parents, to say anything negative about me. He explained this was also attacking our marriage boundaries.

He told us, "You'd be surprised how many people come in here and the love is gone. You both have told me you love each other. That's the most important thing."

Sometimes we get so angry, and we become so consumed with how we feel, or how badly we have been treated, that we forget the basics of WHY we got married. WE LOVE THIS GUY!!!!!!!!

Sit down and write down why you love him, and read it every time you get upset. It helps focus us back to LOVE. Read Songs of Solomon - that's YOUR man talking to YOU!!!

Step moms, your man loves you. *HE LOVES YOU!*

Sometimes men try very hard to "simply get along with everyone", and they don't realize that **sometimes the Enemy can use peacekeepers *to disrupt* peace** - that is why Christ was not a Peace Keeper - but a Peace Maker. There's a big difference!

Matthew 21: 12-13. "Jesus entered the temple area and drove out all who were buying and selling there. He overturned the tables of the money changers and the benches of those selling doves. "It is written," he said to them, "'My house will be called a house of prayer,' but you are making it a 'den of robbers.'"

We also need to be peace makers - and so do our husbands - and sometimes that means shaking the dust off our feet.

Luke 9:5 says "If people do not welcome you, shake the dust off your feet when you leave their town, as a testimony against them."

If someone is saying negative things about you to your husband, that is chipping away at your marital relationship. *Your husband has a covenant with you before God that means he is responsible in the eyes of God to stop this behavior from continuing.* That means telling the stepchildren, the in laws, the ex… whomever it is… that he will no longer listen to these things. They are not life building - they are life draining. **They are not enhancing anyone's lives or hearts. They are only meant to hurt.**

"I'm just being honest," is a phrase I've heard from so many people. We also have an obligation to our men to cut this communication off.

If it is not positive and life building, then we also have a responsibility to stop it. Sometimes that means getting off the phone, not reading emails, and altogether cutting off communication with anyone who cannot respect that this is what you need to do to honor God, and to honor your man and your marriage.

Again, **BE TERRITORIAL** with this. You will see a difference in your relationship when you stop listening to negativity, and you stop participating in it.

Yes - we need to understand where people are coming from - but then we also need to focus on what God's wants for US - in my case, that meant having as little communication as necessary with the ex for a time of healing for our marriage. I needed to understand that she was struggling with suddenly being in town and spending time with Lucas, and that it wasn't going as she'd planned it in her mind. Her relationship with Lucas was damaged, and she was lashing out at Steve and me, trying to make herself not have to look at what the issues really were. She thought she would move to town after seeing Lucas very little over a 6 year period, and that she would be the center of his world. Not only were there many conflicts between Ann and Lucas, but Lucas turned his back on God, got into trouble with drugs again, and started lashing out verbally and physically. And while we listened for a time to Ann and her hurting emotions, we finally had to realize that this was not healthy for us to listen to this.

We limited communication, and Steve stopped answering his phone every time she called. She would leave messages, crying or ranting, but he wouldn't call back. This was not being mean - this was protecting OUR marriage boundary. *If nothing productive is going to come out of a conversation, consider WHY you (or he) need to have that conversation.* Is it just curiosity or a need to have something else to gossip about? Or will it be healthier for you and your man to shake the dust off your feet, and look to the Lord?

YOUR FAMILY

DISCIPLINE:

This is a big issue in blended families. While the law sees the biological parent who has custody as the one who determines and hands out the discipline, scripture also mandates that it be done by "parents". Ephesians 6:1-3 says, "Children, obey your parents in the Lord, for this is right. "Honor your father and mother" - which is the first commandment with a promise - "that it may go well with you and that you may enjoy long life on the earth."

It is absolutely imperative that step moms and their husbands agree on discipline. This seems to be a little easier when the ex is living out of town. Let me explain.

When Lucas came to live with us, he was very rebellious because he had no rules when he lived in his mother's custody. He had no set bedtime, and he ruled the roost. He had no respect for his stepfather, and this was put into place by Lucas' mother. She absolutely forbade the stepfather to discipline Lucas, and so he had no authority in Lucas' eyes. And therefore, demanded no respect.

So when Lucas came to live with us, he was angry that I was going to possess 50% of the discipline power and authority. This was something he had never encountered.

And it wasn't easy with my husband, either. Divorce has a way of making dads, especially, feel guilty, and children quickly recognize that as a way to manipulate their parents into giving in to their every whim.

Lucas was a master at this, even at the young age of 5, when I first met him.

He knew that if Steve felt guilty over Lucas not being with him 100% of the time, that Steve would pull out his wallet, or let him stay up all night, or plan a trip for "just the two of them". This taught Lucas that he was the most important thing in Steve's life, and that was not healthy.

When Lucas came to live with us at age 12, he was accustomed to manipulating both of his parents into doing what he wanted, and he knew how to make his mother give in - just stop talking to her for a short while, and sure enough, she would send money, give an apology when it wasn't warranted, etc. Lucas was in control of both of them.

Further, anytime Lucas needed discipline, there was a major discussion or argument between my husband and me, and the questioning as to whether I was being too hard on Lucas since he wasn't my kid, "just" my step son. The ex perpetuated this feeling, too, telling Steve that, and telling Lucas that.

And what happens then is - if people have convinced themselves of something, it becomes "real" to them. It becomes their "truth", ***even when it is flat out not true!!!***

Steve felt guilty about the divorce, so he assumed Lucas had a tough life, and he assumed I would treat our own children softer than I was suggesting in the discipline on Lucas. The ex felt her own guilt about sending Lucas away, and what better way to make herself feel better than convince herself - and Lucas - that I would never love him the way she does.

And who is hurt in all of it? The child.

It took years for Steve to realize that I was always trying to be fair for Lucas, and do what was right to guide him in our discipline. It took us having two children of our own, and Steve watching me "mom", and seeing first hand that I was firm and consistent in discipline.

The same thing happened in the ex's house. They adopted a baby and had no conflicts between each other on how to discipline! With Lucas, the ex and her husband never agreed on what punishment was okay, and that sparked many, many arguments. But with another child in the midst, suddenly there was agreement - no false beliefs that the step dad was being too hard on their little girl.

When step mom Tracy married Larry, Larry immediately gave her the 50% authority to discipline. That is very rare, and very much a blessing. They agree on discipline, and hand it out as a team. The step children and their own children know and respect that the step mom/ mom is to be obeyed.

This also makes children feel safe. They have boundaries. And most of all, they feel loved and KNOW they are loved.

Many step mothers say they see a visible difference in their step children when they return home from a visit with the ex. When there is no discipline, there are no boundaries, and the children do not feel safe. This causes confusion and anger within the kids. Some step moms refer to it as "deprogramming". We definitely saw this happen.

When Lucas would come back from his mom's, his brow was actually furrowed. He was crabby and angry, and after about 4 days, his spirit would lift. He was pleasant, respectful, and seemed peaceful. He was returning to a house where there was a bedtime, discipline, etc. Again, boundaries show children we care!!

The reason this was happening in her house was fear. The ex could not discipline Lucas because she was fearful that he would not love her anymore, so he walked all over her.

Even after he graduated high school, Lucas successfully controlled his mother. He often was angry at her for calling him "too much". Well, she paid for his cell phone so our opinion was that she was allowed to call him as much as she wanted! Lucas got so upset with her one day that he threw his phone out of his car window and destroyed it. Ann told Lucas she was not going to buy him another phone, and that he had to pay to replace the phone.

But, when Lucas told us this, he snickered, "But she will. I'll give it two days and she won't be able to handle not talking to me. She'll buy me one."

Within ONE day, he had another phone. Lucas had won again. His mom needed to demonstrate some tough love, but she was too afraid he would no longer love or like her.

If your husband is not disciplining his children, look at what is driving him? Is he not disciplining because he truly thinks something doesn't warrant discipline, or does he make this decision based on his fear that the child will not love him?

Fear is not from God.

Proverbs 13:24 says "He who spares the rod hates his son, but he who loves him is careful to discipline him."

If your husband is choosing not to discipline his child because he fears the ex won't let him see the child, stand up against it. Whatever you choose, time out, grounding, taking away a toy, spanking - whatever it is - be consistent and loving. With our little girls, ages 5 and 6, fresh mouths get them time out in their rooms for 20 minutes. When they come out, they immediately say they are sorry, and they are hugged, and we move on. For Lucas, up until he was 18, his car was taken away, because it was SO important to him - ha ha. We, as parents, need to let the children know we are the authority and we love them. When our 5 year old goes to time out, she wants a hug. I give her a hug, tell her I love her, and then ask her why she's in time out. "Because I hit my sister." She understands, and therefore, it's working.

If your man is doubting himself, encourage him that his children love him, but help him in disciplining in a loving manner. If a 2 year old is mouthy, your husband needs to tell him that's not how we speak. Try a time out chair for 2 minutes. But encourage, don't demand. Suggest lovingly, and don't scoff!

I know it's doubly hard when the kids have different discipline in each house, but that is nearly always the case. I have yet to meet a step mom who says both households are in unison on discipline. When Lucas was 18, he was able to successfully manipulate his mom. When he was disciplined at our home, he rushed over there (since she lived only 5 miles away at the time) because he knew how to make her give in. Steve and I don't like this, but we had to give it to God. We do the best we know how, and then have to release Lucas to Him.

Don't get caught up in irritation - we did this for far too long. What we saw was that Lucas actually felt "less" loved by the house that did not discipline. Even though he wanted to get away with things, he felt more "loved" by us because he saw our discipline as "caring" about how he turned out. It's hard to wait that long, but be consistent and the kids WILL get it.

Lucas would say to Steve and me, "I can't get away with anything with you guys!!" That's good. Because *we can't "get away" with anything with God*, either!

Another thing that happens so often is the step children feel they are entitled to criticize the step parents to their biological parents. This should never be allowed! We had a marriage counselor tell us that by Steve allowing Lucas to "vent" about me, he was actually chipping away our marriage by allowing someone/anyone to say negative things about me, the step mom. This was a behavior the ex had also allowed against her husband - she did not do it to be mean. She thought she was allowing Lucas to "talk" to her, but he was undermining her marriage, and was empowering himself to continue disrespecting his step father.

Our marriage counselor suggested that if Lucas was to say anything negative about me again that Steve was to ask him if he would like to speak to both of us at the same time to discuss it so that I would have a chance to defend myself. That did thwart Lucas' need to criticize me to Steve. He started to see that we were a 'team" that he was probably not going to be able to break up.

Normally, if a parent isn't disciplining in this instance, they feel they will lose the child. This was painfully clear with Steve and his ex. They had such animosity for each other that they were vying desperately to get Lucas to "like them better". They even planned vacations at the same time to see which one Lucas would choose - Florida with Steve or a family reunion with Ann. And then they would put Lucas on the spot to choose, which always ended up with one of them accusing the other of manipulating Lucas to choose that side… and they were both at fault!

This has nothing to do with loving and guiding the child the way the Bible says we should - it's all about revenge -sticking it to the ex. And it hurts the child. Children need boundaries to feel safe, and even if you encourage your husband to allow the child to do more with the ex, the child will feel safe and secure that you didn't allow them to be the rope in this tug of war.

One of the hardest things for Steve and I to learn was to tame our tongues. It is still a daily struggle for both of us. When we would hear from Lucas what the ex was saying about us, we defended ourselves, and then wanted to "even the score" with a story about her. Don't do this!!

It took years for us to stop participating in this vicious cycle. Train yourself to say ONLY nice things about the ex to the step child. You don't need to go overboard. Just don't participate in the bashing. Allow it to come from one side only. My neighbor, Cindy, was raised in a broken home, and she distinctly remembers that her mother never said a negative thing about her father. As she grew up, she attained her own opinion of him, but she is still astounded to this day how much strength it must have taken her mom to not criticize him at every turn. And it had a profound impact on her. It's hard. Try it. Let yourself be distracted if the child is sharing some awful opinion the ex has about you. Don't play into that snare. Be godly. Distract the child. Say something nice. Trust me - God will bless you for it! It's self control, self discipline, and godly obedience.

This is YOUR FAMILY. The child is in your house. YOU are in control - with God's help. Be loving. Don't be catty. When you shut your door, leave all the negativity outside. Your child is home. *YOUR CHILD IS HOME.*

Points to Ponder:

"What God has joined together, let no man put asunder."

Who is chipping away at your marital boundaries? Write down who you think it is, and why.

Who would your husband say is chipping away at your marital boundaries? Possibly your
    sounding board?!
Write down why you think that he believes this.

If these people were taken out of your marital relationship - if only to limit communication with them - what do you and your husband think would change?

What do you think the person you mentioned has done to hurt your marriage? Would your husband agree with you? Why or why not?

What does your husband think the person he named has done to your marital relationship? Do you agree with him - why or why not?

> When comparing stories, are you both realizing that you don't like the input of the people you mentioned for the same reasons?
>
> What does this tell you?

Are you both feeling attacked from the outside? Resolve how to strengthen your marriage boundary. (Example: In our case, it took me not communicating at all with the ex, and my husband letting her leave several messages so he could filter which ones truly needed his attention, and which ones were her talking to him about things she needed to rather discuss with her own man.)

Chapter 7:

In this section, we asked the men married to step moms some questions.
The most telling answer was that ALL of the dads surveyed admitted that being a step mom was much harder on their wives that they expected it to be, and **ALL of them said they doubted their wives would marry them if the women knew it was going to be this hard**!!!!

SURVEY for THE HUSBANDS OF STEP MOMS:

1) What do you see as the thing or things your ex does that makes things difficult on your wife?

2) How have you tried to stop these things from occurring?

3) How do you think your wife views your ex? Don't ask her - this is to get YOUR perception. Also, how do you think your ex views your wife?

4) What is the biggest mistake you think your ex has made concerning your wife, and what is the biggest mistake your wife has made concerning your ex? Please also explain why you think this happened in both instances.

5) What is the best thing your wife has done regarding your children?

6) If she could see then what she sees now, do you personally believe your wife would have married you? Or do you think it's been too hard to deal with the step kids and the ex?

7) What do you think your kids think of their step mom? Do you think they make it hard on her sometimes, if so how and why do you think this is?

Here are some answers from the men:
Some things the ex does that makes it difficult on the step mom are:

1) Being late to pick up kids
2) Use the kids to pass along information regarding appointments
3) Encourages children to not like step mom
4) Doesn't discourage disrespect toward step mom
5   Doesn't support step mom, and is critical of the way she does things
6) Doesn't send clothes back after visits
7) Makes up stories about the dad and the step mom
8) Says negative things to father about step mom, but says them in a "nice" way so father doesn't realize at first that it's an attack on his wife... things such as "I think she's too hard on our son, and maybe she doesn't love him……" planting seeds of doubt

How have the dads tried to stop those things above from happening?

1) Tell the ex wife to support the step mom and tried to build up the step mom's involvement in a positive conversation.
2) Tried yelling at ex, and then ignoring her. Some tried to mediate.
3) Told ex parents need to give information to each other, and leave kids out of it.
4) Tell step mom he appreciates her, even if the ex doesn't.
5) Stopped allowing mom to say things about step mom, and ending conversation if it's anything negative regarding his wife.

How do you think your wife views the ex, and how does the ex view your wife?

1 ALL husbands said the ex HATES the step mom.
2) ALL husbands interviewed say the ex is jealous of the step mom.
3) Most men said their wife would prefer to not have to deal with the ex at all.
4) Some men said the step mom views the ex as a failure as a woman and as a mother.

What is the biggest mistake you think your ex has made concerning your wife?

1 Criticizing her to husband's parents based on lies and jealousy.
2) Trying to tear step mom's marriage apart.
3) One man said his wife is tormented with giving up her children and cannot handle it, and because of it, she lashes out at his wife. He believes both women want what's best for the children but are unable to work together to do it.
4) Another man said he believes his ex knows his son was in the best environment when the ex gave him up, but that she is unable to admit it, so she focuses on her dislike for the step mom.

What is the biggest mistake your wife has made concerning your ex?

1) Responding to her emails and not ignoring it.
2) Emailing her.
3) Getting into arguments with her over "stupid issues".
4) She's too vulnerable and gets hurt by what my ex says.

What is the best thing your wife has done regarding your children?

1) Being involved and volunteering in everything she could since the ex was out of town and I traveled a lot.
2) Love my children and try to guide them in church and in the Lord.
3) Being there for me to help me get through the problems.
4) Getting involved in my kids' activities.

If she could see then what she sees now, do you believe your wife would have married you? Or has it been too hard to deal with step children and an ex?

1) ALL MEN said NO - they do not believe their wives would have married them!!!
2) My kids make it hard on her, but they love her. It's just hard for them to show it because they think their mom will be jealous.
3) I didn't realize it would cause my wife so much heartache to deal with my ex. I never wanted her to be hurt like this.

What do you think your kids think of their step mom? Do you think they make it hard on her sometimes, if so, how and why do you think this is?

1) I think he loves her and he says it and shows it but won't when he's in the presence of his "real" mom. He lies about her behind her back.
2) They like her but don't like her telling them what to do.
3) They feel they are betraying their mom if they are nice to her in front of their mom.
4) They love her more than their own mother but won't admit it.
5) They still want their mother and I together.
6) I don't think they purposefully make it hard on my wife. I think circumstances make it hard for them to make both of their women happy.
7) They love her.

The above are just some of the answers the men revealed.

Chapter 8: ANGER: When to say it and when to pray it.

Psalm 4:4
"In your anger, do not sin; when you are on your beds, search your hearts and be silent."
Ephesians 4:26
"In your anger do not sin. Do not let the sun go down while you are still angry, and do not give the devil a foothold."

God knows and expects that we will feel anger. The hard part is reigning it in like the wild horse that it can be, and controlling it.

Both of these passages suggest that we pray as we go to sleep, making our hearts right with the Father. We all have nights when we go to bed with anger on our minds and hearts, but that is what God wants us to overcome!

There are two things He tells us to do with our anger in these passages:

"Search your hearts and be silent."

Even if you have already "said it", God is telling us the time to stop talking about it is the end of the day. I take this literally. God does not want us to dwell on difficulty and anger. He wants us to beat it in a godly manner, and move on. He truly does want us to start each day with contentment and joy, and this is a choice!

Get to a point with the big hurdles that you can tell your husband, "This instance with the ex, the step kids, the in laws - whomever - has angered me. I have expressed my feelings. Now I give it to God. If you need to discuss it further, I am willing, however, I am going to try to let these conflicts end at the end of the day. Tomorrow is a gift from God, and I want to enjoy it, have joy in it, and focus on the good."

I think that passage is also suggesting we search our own hearts honestly. Sometimes it's hard to be honest with ourselves, isn't it?? Maybe it means facing we are feeling threatened by a relationship, in my case, I was feeling a bit threatened by the relationship between the ex and my mother in law. I felt their bond was sitting around criticizing me. Then God told me, "That is the devil tormenting you. Do not listen to that. Focus on the good."

Did it stop the behavior that was hurting me? No. That relationship still exists today, but I have a freedom in Christ that it no longer keeps me in bondage to be the target!

The second thing these passages tell us is "do not give the devil a foothold." The way we perceive our anger determines whether the devil has a foothold in our lives or not. I have a friend who feels so justified in her dislike of the ex that it has become bigger to her than her relationship with Christ. That's how the devil worms his way in there - into our thoughts, our speaking to others, our feelings. If he can convince us that holding on to hatred or bitterness or anger is perfectly acceptable, then the devil has won part of our hearts.

When I realized I was living with a similar stronghold, I had to obey God, and rid myself of it. I felt justified in being angry at the treatment I had received from my husband, the ex, my stepson, and my in laws. And I boiled it all down to the poor step mother who was doing the best she could, and no one would give her a break. Awwww. Poor me..... Ha ha.

Most of us feel this way at times. Ladies, none of us go into this with the plan of making the step kids' lives miserable. I truly believe we go into this with very good intentions! We do the best we can.

I have yet to meet a step mother or a step kid who doesn't say, "When my step kids got into their 30s, they called and thanked me, and apologized for making things hard at times for me." Or, "I was hard on my step dad. I lied about him all the time to my dad just because I didn't want my dad to think I liked him. I was afraid it was a betrayal."

Lucas has actually, at 19, already said part of that. He has lied so much about me, the step mom, and about his step dad, that sometimes the truth is sort of blurry. He's confused about fact and fiction. But one thing he already admits, and that is that he lies. He struggles with this daily. He felt for years that if he liked his step dad, and let Steve know it, that Steve would hate him. And he struggles with loving me, and letting his mom know it. So instead, he lies to her about me, which incites anger within her, and then spreads like wildfire to my in laws when she calls them with the lies.

The lies are like burning embers on very dry leaves. They so quickly ignite, and then the feelings the lies have created - although based on no truth - have started to heat up feverishly.

Suddenly, the spark has become a small fire. Those feelings turn to anger, rage, hatred, etc. And by the time I am confronted, there is such a forest fire burning that a bucket of truth, a small bucket of water - won't even touch or cool the raging inferno!

Most step moms have been there. Carolyn has never been liked by her in laws because they loved the ex, and because of their relationship with the ex, Carolyn has accepted that she will never be the "daughter in law" that she dreamed she would be. Still, she continues to pick up her step son at all his activities while her husband is working. We sacrifice a lot, but God sees it all!

At 19, it was hard for me to realize that Lucas was still reacting as a hurt child. The heartache he still feels over his parents not being together might not fade. I need to lean on God, and trust that He is in control when I am not.

I love the saying, **"Frustration occurs when we try to control what we cannot, and fail to control what we can."**

I cannot control what anyone says about me.

But I can control how I feel about it - with God's help.

Carolyn cannot convince her in laws that she is worth loving and liking. Many step moms have this battle!

When I am feeling attacked, I find unbelievable peace in the Psalms. A calming in His Word.

You see, I believe when all this happens, God is angry that I am unjustly attacked - any step mom. *But I also believe that He expects me to handle it with grace.* He expects me to learn how to ignore gossip, to refuse to listen to it, and then to - oh boy - forgive when there is no apology. This is God teaching me a lesson. **He sees it all- he knows how you feel!!**

I spent years reminding the ex that she owed me an apology for this and that.

That's not my job.

I can't force her into remorse. God can. And you know what, it might never come… and that's ok.

<u>God loves me, and my salvation is in him. It's not in my husband, my step son, the ex, or my in laws. And none of them can take my salvation away!!!!</u>

<u>Praise God for that!!!!!</u>

PRAYING IT:

For years, I struggled with wanting everyone to get along to the point of sometimes extending myself so far backwards that I became a contortionist!

What I mean by that is that I would be hurt by the ex or my step son or my in laws for something they had done or said to me or about me and then with no apology and no extension of kindness from them, I would again and again extend myself to be "the nice one". I would invite the ex to a party we throw for my stepson, or something of that nature. I would apologize to my stepson or my in laws when an apology was not warranted by me. But I so desperately wanted things to be "better" again, that I found myself taking blame for many things that were not mine to own.

Inevitably, the cycle would continue. What I didn't realize is that I was reinforcing bad behavior every time I did this!

I was allowing myself to be treated poorly, and then I was going back for more! I was allowing them to act any way they chose, and then empowering them to do so by taking the full blame.

Until my friend, Terrie Morgan, told me one day, "Dawn, you don't have to please her (the ex). You have to please God. And God is not pleased in seeing you repeatedly hurt. That's why we sometimes have to move on from certain people."

I was choosing to live in oppression by trying so hard to please everyone - I had warped my view of God, making myself believe if I gave in to everyone, God would be pleased with my submission.

I couldn't have been more wrong!!!!

It took me - are you ready for this- 12 years of repeating this cycle before I finally decided to free myself with the help of the Lord.

God is the god of contentment, and even when others hurt us - or worse, **deliberately** try to hurt us, *it's His amazing grace that can give us peace in the most unmerciful of times.*

You see, I was trying to be "friends" with everyone - a people pleaser. And by doing so, I was displeasing God. Sometimes we have to be strong and firm, and make it clearly understood that certain behavior is not going to be accepted.

For my husband and me, it was the ex's behind the back verbal attacks and lies about me to my stepson, to friends, to my in laws… that finally made us shake off our feet.

Luke 9:5 "If people do not welcome you, shake the dust off your feet when you leave their town, as a testimony against them."

I believe this verse can also pertain to us trying to do the right thing, and some *people not wanting us to do the right thing*, or accusing us of not doing the right thing. **God knows our hearts, and he knows our motives**.

As I look back on all the years raising Lucas, I truly did try to do the right thing. No, I was not perfect. But I truly tried to be involved in everything he did because his parents were not around to do it - his mom was out of state and Steve traveled a lot at the time.

But when I would be accused of whatever I did not being enough, I would take it to heart, and it hurt me so deeply because I remember not knowing what more I could possibly do!

What I realized YEARS later, is that the ones accusing me - the ex and my in laws - did not have **true clear knowledge** of all I was doing. They didn't know about all the games and events for Lucas that I attended with two babies in tow. They didn't truly realize how much I helped him with homework, drove him where he needed to go, entertained his friends and fed them all. They didn't hear those parts from Lucas.

Lucas wanted his mom to be part of my in laws circle because he was close to them, but not close to his maternal grandmother. I had to understand that was a "need" Lucas was trying to fill. His method was to say things about me to both his mom and my in laws, and then tell them to talk about me together, and they agreed.

I had to shake the dust off of my feet, and move away from this behavior.

What I did was simple. I stopped communicating with the ex and truly gave it to God.

Within days, I felt freed. After 12 years of letters, calls, emails, etc... suddenly I had no desire to "tell my side of the story" or to refute the latest lie.

And what I saw was that her behavior continued, but it no longer hurt or angered me.

I had - after 12 years - learned to pray it and NOT say it.

And that's allowed me to enter in God's grace in my decision not to participate in conflict.

SAYING IT:

With my man, Steve, it's the other way around - most of the time I can say it AFTER he gets through his cooling off period. We get ourselves into messes when we are confronted with conflict, and IMMEDIATELY want to tell our husbands what to do and how to do it. With Steve, he needs to tell me the latest argument or conflict, and then he needs me to say NOTHING for about 24 hours. He needs me to listen, and then hear him vent over it for a time before I give my opinion. This is tough at times.

But when I was immediately telling him what I thought, he might agree but wasn't ready to. He needed time to digest what the stepson or the ex was doing and why. Then, if I allowed it, he would come to me for a discussion on what I thought was best.

PRAYING IT AND SAYING IT:

The step kids - that is where we need the most divine intervention. Most of the time, we do simply need to pray. But Lucas has also accused me of being too quiet at times when he is angry, and that's when I need to say very little (also a challenge for me! Ha ha)

Let go and let God.

I often hear step moms say that asking the step kids to do things around the house is a frequent source of conflict. And I also hear how the ex, at times, will encourage that to be a conflict. We went through a time after the ex moved 5 miles away from us that she would refuse to allow Lucas to come back for his Sunday afternoon chores, and therefore, Lucas was not receiving his allowance. It was a power play between the ex and my husband, and it was a way to put Lucas square in the middle.

The directive needs to only come from the Dad, regarding his house. Lucas truly didn't mind doing chores - truth be told, he loved the money! But when his mother and father would argue over this, it made him the center of attention and in his mind, the center of the universe.

Any conflict that had him in the middle made him feel important.

We handled it by setting up a time frame. We were no longer going to tell him repeatedly to mow the lawn or do chores. We gave him until 2 pm Sunday afternoon, and if the chores were not completed - for whatever reason - he would not receive allowance. I was taken completely out of the middle, and Steve would watch the clock. This is where we need the men to be the heavys. If your step children are not helping around the house, come up with a time frame, and something they will lose if it's not followed. Don't get exasperated and naggy if it doesn't happen. Think about how small it is, and be matter of fact.

It irritated me for many weeks that Lucas was refusing to do chores and that his mother was reinforcing his rebellion. But when I hired another teen to mow the yard, and he did a great job, and Lucas no longer received allowance - wow - message received! The money we paid Lucas was now going to a kid in his class, and Lucas lost the privilege of getting any money.

Consequences come with sin, and they come with not following rules. If your step kids don't do as they are told, we can still be loving, just firm and enforce punishment.

Steve and I were not ugly about it. We simply told Lucas that Niko would get his chore money from then on.

This was a wonderful way to get the chores done and skip the conflict over it!

The biggest mistake we make in anger is recalling all of the past offenses. Reminding people of their sins - that is Satan coaxing us to do that, and we need to face him and turn him down when he suggests that.

As we said in an earlier chapter, our husbands are the **HUB** - they hear it from all sides.

We, on the other hand, are the target - we get it from all sides - the in laws have distorted views of us, the ex may have a need to dislike us in order to feel better about herself - the step kids feel they are betraying their parent if they don't dislike us at times and shout it from a mountaintop, and our husbands might lash out at us when they just can't listen to it anymore from all of these people vying for his attention, trying to convince him that their story is the one true story he needs to believe. It's exhausting just to think about, let alone live!

Ladies, I know this is such a tough stop - it is so hard to be hated when you want to be loved. I truly believe God allows this to build our character, and to teach us to rely on HIM and not our husbands - and not people in the world - He wants us to handle all situations with grace, and this is so hard to do and so hard to learn when it does hurt so deeply.

Carolyn is a wonderful and strong woman, who whole heartedly embraced her 6 year old stepson, who suffered from ADD and ADHD. When visiting her in laws with her husband and stepson, Carolyn was doing what she always did with her stepson - care for him, make sure he was cared for - food, schedule, etc... she was "momming" him. Her in laws told her husband, "Tell Carolyn she's not his mom."

In laws are a tough breed to face. When they have an ex in their ear, whispering ungodly gossip, suggesting the step mom doesn't like or love the child the way she does, it's human nature for the in laws to worry about or be protective of the child. Unfortunately, this is usually not done with facts or honesty, but through tainted communication that started with a mom feeling inadequate, maybe feeling replaced, feeling jealous... feeling angry. Maybe things are said in a "nice" tone, seemingly innocent but have fangs that sink deep into hearts.

Carolyn was so hurt, hearing this. She was truly doing her best, and wanted her in laws to know that. But they heard tainted information, believed it, let it sink into their opinion of Carolyn, and suddenly she did not have a chance to be a good step mom in their eyes - no matter what she did.

God knows our hearts. ***Even when we get it wrong, He knows our motives and when they are good, he will bless us.***

Carolyn's husband spoke up for her to his parents, reminded them of all she did and does for his son, and then did not allow them to say things of that nature to him regarding his wife.

He had to say it, but Carolyn had to pray it.

As someone who once prided themselves on being able to tell off the best of them - I can tell you - learning to pray it over saying it is hard for us Type As.

But when I kept still, and prayed to God about my hurt and my anger, etc. I saw God move Steve.

I am able to stay out of the conflict because Steve has stood up for me, to the ex, to his son, to my in laws.

He says it while I pray it. **Sometimes God blesses our obedience in silent submission by pushing someone to the forefront to fight the battle *for* us.**

When your man does this, love him and thank him, and encourage him. Make him understand that protecting you and defending your honor matters. Be graceful and loving. Do not be bitter.

Better to be the one talked about than the one doing the talking, don't you think?

Points to Ponder:

This week, look at the people in your life.
To whom do you say it?

Do you believe this is what God wants you to do, or does he want you to pray it instead? Why?

Have you recognized any behaviors within yourself that could be destructive to you? For example, the behavior I mentioned of me taking the blame for many conflicts over the years in order to push peace?

Chapter 9: Stepmoms in the Bible

The word, "step mother" is not used in the Bible, but they are there, and we can relate and learn from their trials and tribulations, the mistakes they made, and the feelings they felt. We'll look at two. Sarah and Bathsheba.

Sarai/Sarah:

Abraham was in his 80s when God told him he and Sarah would conceive a child. They tried and tried, then Sarah tried to help God with His plan in her own way. This happens a lot - people get impatient and try to push God's plan forward with their own timing. Why do we ever think this is a good idea???

Sarai told Abraham to have relations with her servant girl, Hagar, and a child was created. Sarah made herself a step mother! And, as we see, conflicts resulted over and over as Sarah and Hagar argued over and over. This conflict was part of the consequence to the sin Sarah, Abraham and Hagar agreed to commit.

Genesis Chapter 16:

Verse 4 says, "When Hagar knew she was pregnant, she began to despise Sarah."

This angered Sarah, who then started to blame Abraham for her suffering.

She says to Abraham in verse 5, "You are responsible for the wrong I am suffering. I put my servant in your arms, and now that she knows she is pregnant, she despises me. May the Lord judge between you and me."

Sarah became so harsh to Hagar that Hagar ran away.

Listen to this: Verses 7 through 18, "The Angel of the Lord found Hagar near a spring in the desert; it was the spring that is beside the road to Shur. And he said, "Hagar, servant of Sarai, where have you come from, and where are you going?"

"I'm running away from my mistress Sarai," she answered.

Then the angel of the Lord told her, "Go back to your mistress and submit to her." The angel added, "I will so increase your descendants that they will be too numerous to count."

The angel of the Lord also said to her:

"You are now with child
and you will have a son.
You shall name him Ishmael,

for the Lord has heard of your misery.
He will be a wild donkey of a man;
his hand will be against everyone
and everyone's hand against him,
and he will live in hostility
toward all his brothers."

She gave this name to the Lord who spoke to her: "You are the God who sees me," for she said, "I have now seen the One who sees me." That is why the well was called Beer Lahai Roi; it is still there, between Kadesh and Bered.

So Hagar bore Abram a son, and Abram gave the name Ishmael to the son she had borne. Abram was eighty-six years old when Hagar bore him Ishmael.

I think what this passage shows is that Hagar had remorse for her sin, and was seeking forgiveness from the Lord. The Lord heard her and forgave her, and gave her specific instructions that she followed.

What we can learn from Sarah:

1) She knew what God's plan was and yet, she refused to wait upon His timing. She instead tried to make the conception happen in HER timing, and did so through sin. We cannot put God's plan or His timing into place on our own.

2) After her plan turned chaotic, she wanted to blame Abraham and Hagar, and not face her own part in the sin. This caused conflict and frustration, feeling hurt and angry. Have you ever blamed your husband for conflict surrounding his ex and the step children? I know I am guilty of feeling that way.

3) Sarah should have accepted her place in the sin and found remorse, instead she was harsh to Hagar and verbally blamed Abraham.
   Her anger was completely misdirected.
   AND YET,

4) God forgave her! And still blessed her with a child…..

Genesis 17
13 years later:

When Abram was ninety-nine years old, the LORD appeared to him and said, "I am God Almighty; walk before me and be blameless. I will confirm my covenant between me and you and will greatly increase your numbers." Abram fell facedown.

(This shows Abraham's remorse for the sin.)

"God said to him, "As for me, this is my covenant with you: You will be the father of many nations. No longer will you be called Abram; your name will be Abraham, for I have made you a father of many nations. I will make you very fruitful; I will make nations of you, and kings will come from you. I will establish my covenant as an everlasting covenant between me and you and your descendants after you for the generations to come, to be your God and the God of your descendants after you. The whole land of Canaan, where you are now an alien, I will give as an everlasting possession to you and your descendants after you; and I will be their God."

Then God said to Abraham, "As for you, you must keep my covenant, you and your descendants after you for the generations to come. This is my covenant with you and your descendants after you, the covenant you are to keep: Every male among you shall be circumcised. You are to undergo circumcision, and it will be the sign of the covenant between me and you. For the generations to come every male among you who is eight days old must be circumcised, including those born in your household or bought with money from a foreigner—those who are not your offspring. Whether born in your household or bought with your money, they must be circumcised. My covenant in your flesh is to be an everlasting covenant. Any uncircumcised male, who has not been circumcised in the flesh, will be cut off from his people; he has broken my covenant."

God also said to Abraham, "As for Sarai your wife, you are no longer to call her Sarai; her name will be Sarah. *I will bless her and will surely give you a son by her. I will bless her so that she will be the mother of nations; kings of peoples will come from her."*

Abraham fell facedown; he laughed and said to himself, "Will a son be born to a man a hundred years old? Will Sarah bear a child at the age of ninety?" And Abraham said to God, "If only Ishmael might live under your blessing!"

Then God said, "Yes, but your wife Sarah will bear you a son, and you will call him Isaac. I will establish my covenant with him as an everlasting covenant for his descendants after him. And as for Ishmael, I have heard you: I will surely bless him; I will make him fruitful and will greatly increase his numbers. He will be the father of twelve rulers, and I will make him into a great nation. But my covenant I will establish with Isaac, whom Sarah will bear to you by this time next year." When he had finished speaking with Abraham, God went up from him.

On that very day Abraham took his son Ishmael and all those born in his household or bought with his money, every male in his household, and circumcised them, as God told him. Abraham was ninety-nine years old when he was circumcised, and his son Ishmael was thirteen; Abraham and his son Ishmael were both circumcised on that same day. And every male in Abraham's household, including those born in his household or bought from a foreigner, was circumcised with him.

Think about this!!! 13 years later and that's when it appears Abraham and Sarah were remorseful and finally repentant for the sin, and God blessed them. 13 years!! Oh, how I hope I don't hold on to loving my sins that long....... And notice how loving God is - he blessed Ishmael at Abraham's request, too.

Genesis 18:

The LORD appeared to Abraham near the great trees of Mamre while he was sitting at the entrance to his tent in the heat of the day. Abraham looked up and saw three men standing nearby. When he saw them, he hurried from the entrance of his tent to meet them and bowed low to the ground.

He said, "If I have found favor in your eyes, my lord, do not pass your servant by. Let a little water be brought, and then you may all wash your feet and rest under this tree. Let me get you something to eat, so you can be refreshed and then go on your way—now that you have come to your servant."

"Very well," they answered, "do as you say."

So Abraham hurried into the tent to Sarah. "Quick," he said, "get three seahs of fine flour and knead it and bake some bread."

Then he ran to the herd and selected a choice, tender calf and gave it to a servant, who hurried to prepare it. He then brought some curds and milk and the calf that had been prepared, and set these before them. While they ate, he stood near them under a tree.

"Where is your wife Sarah?" they asked him.

"There, in the tent," he said.

Then the Lord said, "I will surely return to you about this time next year, and Sarah your wife will have a son."

Now Sarah was listening at the entrance to the tent, which was behind him. Abraham and Sarah were already old and well advanced in years, and Sarah was past the age of childbearing. So Sarah laughed to herself as she thought, "After I am worn out and my master is old, will I now have this pleasure?"

Then the Lord said to Abraham, "Why did Sarah laugh and say, 'Will I really have a child, now that I am old?' Is anything too hard for the Lord? I will return to you at the appointed time next year and Sarah will have a son."

Sarah was afraid, so she lied and said, "I did not laugh."

But he said, "Yes, you did laugh."

When I read this passage, it is so amazing! Sitting down with the Lord and listening to the Lord telling Abraham what he will do for him! And Sarah is listening and laughing at the Lord promising her a child???? Will she ever learn? Will any of us? How often has the Lord told you something and you scoff at it because your human nature is to doubt that YOU can do it? The Lord can do it THROUGH you. That's His glory. Where is the glory if you can do it on your own without His help? Where is His glory, then?

He is mightiest when he uses us when we are weakest and lowliest. He doesn't need heroes. He needs us to be faithful and obedient.

And more victory!

Hebrew 11:11-13 - God's glory is shown even after big mistakes! Sarah waited 90 years to conceive a baby!

Hebrews 11:

By faith Abraham, even though he was past age—and Sarah herself was barren—was enabled to become a father because he considered him faithful who had made the promise. And so from this one man, and he as good as dead, came descendants as numerous as the stars in the sky and as countless as the sand on the seashore.

All these people were still living by faith when they died. ***They did not receive the things promised; they only saw them and welcomed them from a distance.*** And they admitted that they were aliens and strangers on earth. People who say such things show that they are looking for a country of their own. If they had been thinking of the country they had left, they would have had opportunity to return. Instead, they were longing for a better country—a heavenly one. Therefore God is not ashamed to be called their God, for he has prepared a city for them.

Abraham's descendants did not see the promises, but they were content in the fact that God promised them, and therefore, they were faithful. Are we so faithful when we want what we want and don't want to wait on God's perfect timing? When we force the timing, and take God out of the equation, we throw ourselves into chaos. That's what happened to Sarah and Abraham - 13 years of chaos until remorse finally settled in and God's blessing reigned down. Do you ever feel that way? That there is chaos with your husband, the ex and your step children? Do you think that is a consequence to the sin of divorce? I think it might be. God forgives us, but we still have to deal with the consequences to sin.

Bathsheba:

David had an affair with Bathseba while she was married to Uriah.

2 Samuel 11

"In the spring, at the time when kings go off to war, David sent Joab out with the king's men and the whole Israelite army. They destroyed the Ammonites and besieged Rabbah. But David remained in Jerusalem.

One evening David got up from his bed and walked around on the roof of the palace. From the roof he saw a woman bathing. The woman was very beautiful, and David sent someone to find out about her. The man said, "Isn't this Bathsheba, the daughter of Eliam and the wife of Uriah the Hittite?" Then David sent messengers to get her. She came to him, and he slept with her. (She had purified herself from her uncleanness.) Then she went back home. The woman conceived and sent word to David, saying, "I am pregnant."

So David sent this word to Joab: "Send me Uriah the Hittite." And Joab sent him to David. When Uriah came to him, David asked him how Joab was, how the soldiers were and how the war was going. Then David said to Uriah, "Go down to your house and wash your feet." So Uriah left the palace, and a gift from the king was sent after him. But Uriah slept at the entrance to the palace with all his master's servants and did not go down to his house.

When David was told, "Uriah did not go home," he asked him, "Haven't you just come from a distance? Why didn't you go home?"

Uriah said to David, "The ark and Israel and Judah are staying in tents, and my master Joab and my lord's men are camped in the open fields. How could I go to my house to eat and drink and lie with my wife? As surely as you live, I will not do such a thing!"

Then David said to him, "Stay here one more day, and tomorrow I will send you back." So Uriah remained in Jerusalem that day and the next. At David's invitation, he sleep on his mat among his master's servants; he did not go home.

In the morning David wrote a letter to Joab and sent it with Uriah. In it he wrote, "Put Uriah in the front line where the fighting is fiercest. Then withdraw from him so he will be struck down and die."

So while Joab had the city under siege, he put Uriah at a place where he knew the strongest defenders were. When the men of the city came out and fought against Joab, some of the men in David's army fell; moreover, Uriah the Hittite died.

Joab sent David a full account ate and drank with him, and David made him drunk. But in the evening Uriah went out to of the battle. He instructed the messenger: "When you have finished giving the king this account of the battle, the king's anger may flare up, and he may ask you, 'Why did you get so close to the city to fight? Didn't you know they would shoot arrows from the wall? Who killed Abimelech son of Jerub-Besheth ? Didn't a woman throw an upper millstone on him from the wall, so that he died in Thebez? Why did you get so close to the wall?' If he asks you this, then say to him, 'Also, your servant Uriah the Hittite is dead.' "

The messenger set out, and when he arrived he told David everything Joab had sent him to say. The messenger said to David, "The men overpowered us and came out against us in the open, but we drove them back to the entrance to the city gate. Then the archers shot arrows at your servants from the wall, and some of the king's men died. Moreover, your servant Uriah the Hittite is dead."

David told the messenger, "Say this to Joab: 'Don't let this upset you; the sword devours one as well as another. Press the attack against the city and destroy it.' Say this to encourage Joab."

When Uriah's wife heard that her husband was dead, she mourned for him. After the time of mourning was over, David had her brought to his house, and she became his wife and bore him a son. ***But the thing David had done displeased the LORD***."

David had a plan to meet his selfish desires. He took another man's wife, and then had the man killed. Bathsheba also sinned, committing adultery with David.

The decisions they made had huge consequences. The decisions we make also have consequences. When we deceive, it snowballs, and soon the plan we have created becomes a snare for ourselves.

Then, at times, the Lord sends someone to correct us in our wrongdoing. How do we accept this? Read on to see how David faced being confronted with his sins.

2 Samuel 12

"The Lord sent Nathan to David. When he came to him, he said, "There were two men in a certain town, one rich and the other poor. The rich man had a very large number of sheep and cattle, but the poor man had nothing except one little ewe lamb he had bought.

He raised it, and it grew up with him and his children. It shared his food, drank from his cup and even slept in his arms. It was like a daughter to him.

"Now a traveler came to the rich man, but the rich man refrained from taking one of his own sheep or cattle to prepare a meal for the traveler who had come to him. Instead, he took the ewe lamb that belonged to the poor man and prepared it for the one who had come to him."

David burned with anger against the man and said to Nathan, "As surely as the Lord lives, the man who did this deserves to die! He must pay for that lamb four times over, because he did such a thing and had no pity."

Then Nathan said to David, **"You are the man!** This is what the Lord, the God of Israel, says: 'I anointed you king over Israel, and I delivered you from the hand of Saul. I gave your master's house to you, and your master's wives into your arms. I gave you the house of Israel and Judah. And if all this had been too little, I would have given you even more. Why did you despise the word of the Lord by doing what is evil in his eyes? You struck down Uriah the Hittite with the sword and took his wife to be your own. You killed him with the sword of the Ammonites. Now, therefore, **the sword will never depart from your house**, because you despised me and took the wife of Uriah the Hittite to be your own.'

"This is what the Lord says: '**Out of your own household I am going to bring calamity upon you.** Before your very eyes I will take your wives and give them to one who is close to you, and he will lie with your wives in broad daylight. You did it in secret, but I will do this thing in broad daylight before all Israel.' "

Then David said to Nathan, "I have sinned against the Lord."

Nathan replied, "The Lord has taken away your sin. You are not going to die. But because by doing this you have made the enemies of the Lord show utter contempt, **the son born to you will die**."

After Nathan had gone home, the Lord struck the child that Uriah's wife had borne to David, and he became ill. David pleaded with God for the child. He fasted and went into his house and spent the nights lying on the ground. The elders of his household stood beside him to get him up from the ground,

but he refused, and he would not eat any food with them.

On the seventh day the child died. David's servants were afraid to tell him that the child was dead, for they thought, "While the child was still living, we spoke to David but he would not listen to us. How can we tell him the child is dead? He may do something desperate."

David noticed that his servants were whispering among themselves and he realized the child was dead. "Is the child dead?" he asked.

"Yes," they replied, "he is dead."

Then David got up from the ground. After he had washed, put on lotions and changed his clothes, he went into the house of the Lord and worshiped. Then he went to his own house, and at his request they served him food, and he ate.

His servants asked him, "Why are you acting this way? While the child was alive, you fasted and wept, but now that the child is dead, you get up and eat!"

He answered, "While the child was still alive, I fasted and wept. I thought, 'Who knows? The Lord may be gracious to me and let the child live.' But now that he is dead, why should I fast? Can I bring him back again? I will go to him, but he will not return to me."

Then David comforted his wife Bathsheba, and he went to her and lay with her. She gave birth to a son, and they named him Solomon. The Lord loved him; and because the Lord loved him, he sent word through Nathan the prophet to name him Jedidiah."

There are many things we as step moms need to understand in this former passage. Because of his sin against God (which is all sin), God took David and Bathsheba's baby. It took discipline of this magnitude to get David's attention and make him repentant! God's message - "...the sword will never depart from your house", and "Out of your household I will bring calamity..." is foreshadowing of the trouble and turmoil David's children would cause him. One son raped his own half sister. They also committed murder. David's family was filled with turmoil.

Could this be a consequence to the sin?

David had learned true remorse through this pain, and seeing this, we read that "God loved him." God then blessed David and Bathsheba with a son, Solomon.

This is encouraging to us that God blesses us as step moms, he blesses our unions in marriage ***as long as our eyes are fixed upon Him***. When David tried to get what he wanted in his own way, his son was taken from him. When David and Bathsheba found remorse, God again was ready to bless them!

David had many wives. When I think of how difficult it is sometimes to be a step mother and the trials we go through in getting along with everyone surrounding my husband's divorce, I think of David's family.

David had many wives, many concubines, and many children.

Here are some of David's wives:

*1) Michal had no children. She was taken away from David by her father, Saul, and married another man. Then David bought her back while she was still married to that other man.

2 Samuel 14 and 15 says, "Then David sent messengers to Ish-Bosheth son of Saul, demanding, "Give me my wife Michal, whom I have betrothed to myself for the price of a hundred Philistine foreskins." So Ish-Bosheth gave orders and had her taken away from her husband Paltiel son of Laish."

2 Samuel later describes how Michal despised David. She became bitter over her life and resented David's relationship with God. After her first marriage with David, he married Ahinoam and Abigail. And then sent for Michal again.

*2) Ahinoam had Amnon, David's first born son.

*3) Abigail - Her first husband was Nabal.

Nabal died and David sent a messenger to ask Abigail to become his wife. She agreed. David had also just married Ahinoam, as well.

Abigail did not have children with David, although she had a son from Nabal.

*4) Maacah gave birth to Absalom and Tamar. Absalom was wild, sinned and did not seek forgiveness, brought heartache to David. Tamar was David's only daughter.

(She was raped by her half brother and another brother then had that brother murdered for it.)

*5) Haggith had Adonijah - he tried to steal David's throne from Solomon, Bathsheba's son.

And the number of wives continued to grow:

2 Samuel 5:13 "After he left Hebron, David took more concubines and wives in Jerusalem, and more sons and daughters were born to him. These are the names of the children born to him there: Shammua, Shobab, Nathan, Solomon, Ibhar, Elishua, Nepheg, Japhia, Elishama, Eliada, and Eliphelet.

*Then he met Bathsheba. After their first baby was taken by the Lord as a consequence for their sin, she gave birth to Solomon.

Imagine what it was like being one of many wives. Can you imagine the visitation schedule that David might have been forced into during this day and age?!

Do you think the women got along? When you consider how difficult it is to deal with an ex at times, consider the possibility that David's wives didn't deal with exes - they dealt with many wives at the same time! Most with children, most living in the palace together! Imagine sharing your husband with many wives....

Bathsheba was a step mom to at least 14 children! And she had to deal with at least 6 wives who are named in the Bible, and a list that is inferred of more wives who are not named! Think about that when you're having a hard time dealing with one! Ha ha.

And yet, in 1 Kings, when Adonijah was trying to steal David's throne, David honored a promise he had made to Bathsheba many years earlier. In spite of his many wives and concubines, David and Bathsheba clearly had a unique relationship - perhaps in their sin and the consequences to that sin of losing their baby - their remorse bound them. She is a mother and stepmother, and David honored his promise and made their son, Solomon, king.

1 Kings 1:

Starting with verse 28: Then King David said, "Call in Bathsheba." So she came into the king's presence and stood before him.

The king then took an oath: "As surely as the Lord lives, who has delivered me out of every trouble, I will surely carry out today what I swore to you by the Lord, the God of Israel: Solomon your son shall be king after me, and he will sit on my throne in my place."

Then Bathsheba bowed low with her face to the ground and, kneeling before the king, said, "May my lord King David live forever!"

King David said, "Call in Zadok the priest, Nathan the prophet and Benaiah son of Jehoiada." When they came before the king, he said to them: "Take your lord's servants with you and set Solomon my son on my own mule and take him down to Gihon. There have Zadok the priest and Nathan the prophet anoint him king over Israel. Blow the trumpet and shout, 'Long live King Solomon!' Then you are to go up with him, and he is to come and sit on my throne and reign in my place. I have appointed him ruler over Israel and Judah."

Benaiah son of Jehoiada answered the king, "Amen! May the Lord, the God of my lord the king, so declare it. As the Lord was with my lord the king, so may he be with Solomon to make his throne even greater than the throne of my lord King David!"

David's promise to Bathsheba was honored. Solomon became king. I wonder what the other moms and step moms married to David thought about that! I wonder if there was any bickering, or complaining??

Let's remember Sarah and Bathsheba (and all the other step moms David created!) and learn from them.

Forgiveness does not remove the consequences of sin. Yet, still we have hope!

I can't think of a better time to remember what we are to dwell upon - the fruit of the spirit.

When things get rough and you want to bicker or complain, or you are feeling attacked, speak out loud the fruit of the spirit, as you give praise to God in all things, and find joy in every circumstance…. As hard as it is. Remembering that "the testing of your faith produces patience."

God is changing our character to give Him glory - NOT to glorify ourselves.

One of the hardest things to realize is that we are tested every time something goes wrong in our lives - how we handle it, how we think about it, how we talk about it - all of it needs to glorify God - and not the world.

Galatians 5:22-23:

But the fruit of the Spirit is **love, joy, peace, patience, kindness, goodness, faithfulness, gentleness and self-control**. Against such things there is no law.

Chapter 10: Moving on from the Mess ups

As parents, we make mistakes. As people, we make mistakes. But what I experienced as a step mom was unlike any mistake I ever made in my entire life! In every single other instance in my life, there was confession and forgiveness. There were no bridges that weren't rebuilt or mended.

But step motherhood is different.

When I made a mistake, as many other step moms have told me, it never was erased from the blackboard that my in laws, my step son, and the ex were keeping on me. It was a scoreboard that never was cleared. Knowing this condemnation exists, many of us step moms think and OVER think nearly everything we do when it comes to the ex, the step kids, and the in laws.

We become almost obsessive in trying to guess how anyone could possibly see this or that, and worrying what everyone will think.

Once my stepson lied to his mom about me driving halfway to meet her. He desperately wanted her to prove to him how much she loved him and wanted her to drive 10 hours to prove it. I had offered to drive 5 hours to meet her. When Lucas became angry with me for asking him to vacuum our SUV, he called his mom and told her I was refusing to drive him halfway the following day, and that she had to come all the way. This was a lie. After everything was worked out that same night, Lucas wrote me a very kind two page letter, apologizing to me and asking for forgiveness. Steve sent a copy of this letter to the ex (after I drove 5 hours to meet her). He did this for my benefit because she immediately believed Lucas' lies about me, and was furious with me, even though I had done nothing.

We both thought if she read the honesty and sincerity in Lucas' letter that she would realize she had falsely accused me of ever refusing to drive halfway.

To our shock, she instead wrote Steve an email saying I was the one who should have written Lucas an apology letter!

Ladies, this is so common. When people want to think the worst of people for whatever reason, it doesn't take much for them to find a reason to reinforce their feelings, **even if that reason is purely in their own minds**.

<u>**I never expected to be hated so much just for caring for and loving a child**</u>, and raising him when his mother sent him to live with us. I had a much rosier picture in my head on how it would all go!!

One time when Lucas was in trouble with drugs and grounded, he began swearing at me. When he refused to stop swearing, and continued to throw his bedroom door open so I could hear him, I slapped him across the face. He lunged at me and took me to the ground.

I should not have slapped him. That is true. I should have walked away.

But what I then lived through was my stepson and the ex twisting it into something that was so out of context that it literally made me dizzy at one point when my husband was explaining how twisted the truth had become.

For the next two weeks, I allowed myself to live under guilt and condemnation in the shadow of sadness, and despair.

I felt like an awful person and blamed myself for not walking away. I truly felt I had let Christ down so much that I had a very hard time "snapping out of it".

Romans 8 helped me remember who I am in Christ.

Romans 8:1-17
Life Through the Spirit
"Therefore, there is now no condemnation for those who are in Christ Jesus, because through Christ Jesus the law of the Spirit of life set me free from the law of sin and death. For what the law was powerless to do in that it was weakened by the sinful nature, God did by sending his own Son in the likeness of sinful man to be a sin offering. And so he condemned sin in sinful man, in order that the righteous requirements of the law might be fully met in us, who do not live according to the sinful nature but according to the Spirit.

Those who live according to the sinful nature have their minds set on what that nature desires; but those who live in accordance with the Spirit have their minds set on what the Spirit desires. The mind of sinful man is death, but the mind controlled by the Spirit is life and peace; the sinful mind is hostile to God. It does not submit to God's law, nor can it do so. Those controlled by the sinful nature cannot please God.

You, however, are controlled not by the sinful nature but by the Spirit, if the Spirit of God lives in you. And if anyone does not have the Spirit of Christ, he does not belong to Christ. But if Christ is in you, your body is dead because of sin, yet your spirit is alive because of righteousness. And if the Spirit of him who raised Jesus from the dead is living in you, he who raised Christ from the dead will also give life to your mortal bodies through his Spirit, who lives in you.

Therefore, brothers, we have an obligation—but it is not to the sinful nature, to live according to it. For if you live according to the sinful nature, you will die; but if by the Spirit you put to death the misdeeds of the body, you will live, because those who are led by the Spirit of God are sons of God. For you did not receive a spirit that makes you a slave again to fear, but you received the Spirit of sonship. And by him we cry, "Abba, Father." The Spirit himself testifies with our spirit that we are God's children. Now if we are children, then we are heirs—heirs of God and co-heirs with Christ, if indeed we share in his sufferings in order that we may also share in his glory."

I especially love verse 15 - **"For you did not receive a spirit that makes you a slave again to fear..."**

It reminded me that if I mess up and miss one of the rungs on that ladder, I can still continue the climb. Each day I try again. And again. And pray for guidance to get better at it. And I will fall again, but I will get back up.

My motives with Lucas for years have been good. I wanted him to be happy, godly, safe, secure, and I wanted it because I thought I was doing the right thing. My motives were not to show anyone up - they were to raise a well adjusted child. And God knows that - HE knows my heart.

Step moms, He knows your hearts! He knows you don't deliberately want to cause conflict with the ex, the step kids, your husband, the in laws - or anyone. He knows that! He blesses us when our motives are pure.

He also knows we all have a sinful nature and if we fall to it, ***which he expects,*** He is right there to forgive us and get us going again!

And when we mess up, like I did, he forgives us WHEN WE ARE TRULY REMORSEFUL.

Do not live under guilt and condemnation. There is a time to confess, "I messed up."

And there is a time to talk it over with God. But then God expects us to get up and move on. If someone reminds you of your wrongs, don't get angry and don't push yourself back into that guilty place of feeling condemned.

You are forgiven in Christ, and if someone in the world chooses not to forgive you, remember that they answer to God. You have already answered to Him, in your confession and obedience. If they do not forgive you, they are choosing to also not have their sins forgiven by God.

Mark 11:25-26.

"And when you stand praying, if you hold anything against anyone, forgive him, so that your Father in heaven may forgive you your sins. But if you do not forgive, neither will your Father who is in heaven forgive your sins."

And if Christ forgives you, who in the world has the power to NOT forgive you and hold it against you? No one!! **If someone is choosing not to forgive you, they are choosing to sin against God.**

And *every time* **He forgives** - when we are truly remorseful - listen to Luke 7:37-48, and be encouraged.

"Now one of the Pharisees invited Jesus to have dinner with him, so he went to the Pharisee's house and reclined at the table. When a woman who had lived a sinful life in that town learned that Jesus was eating at the Pharisee's house, she brought an alabaster jar of perfume, and as she stood behind him at his feet weeping, she began to wet his feet with her tears. Then she wiped them with her hair, kissed them and poured perfume on them.

When the Pharisee who had invited him saw this, he said to himself, "If this man were a prophet, he would know who is touching him and what kind of woman she is—that she is a sinner."

Jesus answered him, "Simon, I have something to tell you."

"Tell me, teacher," he said.

"Two men owed money to a certain moneylender. One owed him five hundred denarii, and the other fifty. Neither of them had the money to pay him back, so he canceled the debts of both. Now which of them will love him more?"

Simon replied, "I suppose the one who had the bigger debt canceled."

"You have judged correctly," Jesus said.

Then he turned toward the woman and said to Simon, "Do you see this woman? I came into your house. You did not give me any water for my feet, but she wet my feet with her tears and wiped them with her hair. You did not give me a kiss, but this woman, from the time I entered, has not stopped kissing my feet. You did not put oil on my head, but she has poured perfume on my feet. Therefore, I tell you, her many sins have been forgiven—for she loved much. But he who has been forgiven little loves little."

Then Jesus said to her, "Your sins are forgiven."

Yes - be forgiven - accept the forgiveness. Love MUCH! Don't love little!

After that above mentioned argument, Lucas became empowered with his mom's verbal attacks upon me, and he began to manipulate my husband with his lies. God had forgiven me, but the Devil was still trying to torment me with that. Until I poured myself into His Word, and strengthened myself with the knowledge of who I am in Christ, I could not pull out of it.

Once I reinforced my heart and mind with the TRUTH in God's Word, I saw amazing things happen.

Steve's heart softened and with no reason, he dismissed Lucas' verbal attacks upon me. Without me saying a thing, God was removing the scales from Steve's eyes, and he was seeing Lucas and his manipulation clearly - WITHOUT ME SAYING A WORD!

You see, Lucas had not gone to God and confessed his role in the argument, nor had he any remorse for swearing repeatedly at me or hurting me physically. His mom had empowered that with a sinful nature, rather than talking it over with God. When this happens, and we take our hearts to God, **He protects us divinely**. And as long we are obedient and stay in His word, YOU WILL SEE IT.

Now the hard part becomes pride.

When we are remorseful and accept God's forgiveness, we have to continue to be wise in Him, and not ourselves.

It's easy at this point to also fall into the "Well, sure, I made mistakes but look at what you've done and not asked for forgiveness of me....."

Part of me certainly has wanted to do that with Lucas, the ex, and my in laws.

But God is pruning us to be forgivers when it doesn't make sense, and that is hard!!

It's similar to what Michal, David's wife, did to her life - she was very bitter that David took her back as his wife after she was married to Paltiel. She was angry with David - the Bible says her heart despised him. She chose bitterness. She chose not to forgive.

When we face tough circumstances, react as though you are literally standing next to Christ, and that you are being tested in your reaction.

In my situation, it was difficult for me to seek forgiveness from the ex or my stepson and then receive no apologies from them for the wrongs they committed against me. But I chose (after therapy and good friends Biblical encouragement!) To forgive when it didn't make sense.

Yes, I forgave, and it was HARD! But I also started to see - through Lucas' stories - how bitterness was alive and well in his mom's house… and hearing about the complaining and the sorrow made me realize I needed to break free from that prison, too!

That's about the time I started speaking it into my life with God's help.

"Yes, Lord, I forgive her."

"Yes, Lord, thank you for forgiving me."

"Lord, loose the spirit of healing on both our households. Lord, help me be a better wife, mom and step mom."

"Help me to LOVE as you command."

If you ask the Lord what to do, He will tell you. He promised us that in Isaiah.

Isaiah 30:21 "Whether you turn to the right or to the left, your ears will hear a voice behind you, saying, "This is the way: walk in it."

If you are truly seeking God, he will always show you the right way. You WILL hear Him.

I love the saying, **"A smart man gets lots of advice. A wise man weighs the advice he gets."**

I think it's great to talk to godly people who will guide you in a godly fashion, but we need to remember that Christ is the counselor we need to turn to every single time. We need to talk, to ask, to seek, to lean on HIM. His Word is there for us - for our strength and guidance.

He will nudge us in the right direction if we are truly seeking Him, and not seeking an answer that we have already determined we would like to hear.

Let's be more encouraged in the hard times when our step kids are giving us a hard time - or we are giving the ex a hard time - or any combination.

Let's read the Sermon on the Mount - where do you fit in? Do you thirst for righteousness? I know I did. Are you poor in spirit? Do you mourn for your marriage at times? Are you feeling persecuted? Most step moms feel all of these at some point.

But listen to the good news!

You WILL be shown mercy - you WILL be comforted - you WILL be a son of God - you WILL see God - the kingdom of heaven IS YOURS!

It doesn't say "You *might* feel better. You *may* have some support…"

God is not a god who waivers. He stands firm and he is definitive and deliberate with how he feels about you and what he wants for you, FOR YOU, A STEPMOM!

Matthew 5:1-12
Sermon on the Mount
"Now when he saw the crowds, he went up on a mountainside and sat down. His disciples came to him, and he began to teach them saying:

"Blessed are the poor in spirit,
for theirs is the kingdom of heaven.

Blessed are those who mourn,
for they will be comforted.

Blessed are the meek,
for they will inherit the earth.

Blessed are those who hunger and thirst for righteousness,
for they will be filled.

Blessed are the merciful,
for they will be shown mercy.

Blessed are the pure in heart,
for they will see God.

Blessed are the peacemakers,
for they will be called sons of God.

Blessed are those who are persecuted because of righteousness,
for theirs is the kingdom of heaven.

"Blessed are you when people insult you, persecute you and falsely say all kinds of evil against you because of me. **Rejoice and be glad**, because great is your reward in heaven, for in the same way they persecuted the prophets who were before you."

Rejoice when people say false things about you…. This is a test. I am challenged by this. Rejoice in this when people lie about you! I have yet to meet a step mom that hasn't been the victim of lies from the ex, the step kids, or the in laws. It hurts. It is hard. And yet, God tells us to REJOICE!

And here's more encouragement: We are More than Conquerors!

Romans 8:28-39

"And we know that in all things God works for the good of those who love him, who have been called according to his purpose. For those God foreknew he also predestined to be conformed to the likeness of his Son, that he might be the firstborn among many brothers. And those he predestined, he also called; those he called, he also justified; those he justified, he also glorified.

What, then, shall we say in response to this? **If God is for us, who can be against us?** He who did not spare his own Son, but gave him up for us all—how will he not also, along with him, graciously give us all things? Who will bring any charge against those whom God has chosen? It is God who justifies. Who is he that condemns? Christ Jesus, who died—more than that, who was raised to life—is at the right hand of God and is also interceding for us. Who shall separate us from the love of Christ? Shall trouble or hardship or persecution or famine or nakedness or danger or sword? As it is written:

"For your sake we face death all day long; we are considered as sheep to be slaughtered." No, in all these things we are more than conquerors through him who loved us. For I am convinced that neither death nor life, neither angels nor demons, neither the present nor the future, nor any powers, neither height nor depth, nor anything else in all creation, will be able to separate us from the love of God that is in Christ Jesus our Lord."

Nothing can separate us from the LOVE OF GOD! Nothing. Not a lie about us, not a bad attitude from a step kid, not an unkind word from anyone, *not even any of our own mess ups* - NOTHING CAN SEPARATE US FROM THE LOVE OF GOD.

Dwell upon that. Remember that. Your salvation is in Christ, not any man.

Points to Ponder:

Have you not forgiven yourself for something? Something you said to the ex, to your step kids, etc? Something you did?

Cleanse yourself before your Savior. Get your heart right with God. Confess it to Him, and to anyone you feel you may have wronged. God sees your motives and will bless you for trying to make things right. Even if it is in your mind control. Are you thinking in a way that is displeasing to the Father? Confess it to Him - he already knows, and he wants to help you overcome it.

If he is nudging you right now about something, he wants you to move on from it, grow from it, so he can prune you and help you grow in Christ.

Chapter 11: WHAT NOW?
Living in VICTORY!

Number 1: The WORD.

Ihonestly don't think I could make it without the Bible. When I am weak, it strengthens me. When I am down, it encourages me.

We sometimes forget that it is THE WORD OF GOD. Think about that - the **word** of GOD!

If we don't literally "hear" God, we can read His words to us. How amazing that is. Dwell upon how awesome our God is that he has a love letter and a life manual all in one - just for us!

Staying in a bible study is crucial for us to grow in our walk with Christ, and to learn how to focus on and produce the fruit of the Spirit. The second we start a day by our own strength and with our own control, things will be difficult. I challenge you to put this to the test.

Start a day without God.

Keep a journal that day on what goes wrong, how you felt, how you dealt with circumstances.

The following day, start the day praising God, reading his Word, praying. I believe you will see a drastic change in YOUR attitude - maybe not those around you - but you WILL feel differently. I challenge you to face the trials of life in a godly way, and I believe you will end that day with a different perspective.... All because you trusted God - not yourself - to get you through the simple and yet, tough challenges of a day.

Galatians 5:22-26 says "But the fruit of the Spirit is love, joy, peace, patience, kindness, goodness, faithfulness, gentleness and self-control. Against such things there is no law. Those who belong to Christ Jesus have crucified the sinful nature with its passions and desires. Since we live by the Spirit, let us keep in step with the Spirit. Let us not become conceited, provoking and envying each other."

Number 2: The FRUIT:

Identify where the fruit is alive in your life: Be bold. Are you kind on a regular basis? Are you known for your patience? Are you gentle to everyone? The fruit cannot only be considered when dealing with people we love. On the contrary - **our true fruit is demonstrated to God in how we handle the difficult people.** As step moms, we are faced with many trials and tribulations that many other moms may have to face.

You can't control the ex - but you can control how you react to what she does, what the kids say she does (because it might not be true!), what she says and what the kids say she says.

When we were planning Lucas' graduation party, Steve had planned on not inviting his ex, as she was planning her own party. It was brought to our attention that she wanted to come to our party. I was torn, and asked many Christian friends and Christian step moms what they would do. I finally told my husband that it was up to him. Whatever he decided was fine. He told me, "There are people who would make it a point NOT to invite the ex, and YOU are not that type of person. Leave it to you to invite her, in spite of everything that's happened."

The reason this was so shocking to me was that I was internally struggling with what I did want - but my husband had faith in me to be a godly person and a godly example! It really choked me up, and I don't think he realizes the compliment that was to me.

Guess what happened? Turns out she didn't want to come, in the first place. But she was hoping we would ban her from coming, so we would look mean. But God was in control, and he blessed Steve and I for simple obedience *that really wasn't that simple*!

God will tell you the right thing to do - He always does. And sometimes, it's simply offering something that He has no intention of allowing to happen, but he still wants our submission.

If we had not been obedient, there would have been chaos - anger on our part, on her part, probably on my stepson's part, and that would have been us clinging to a sinful nature. That's exactly what God wants us to identify and rid ourselves of - one day at a time. Dwell upon each fruit, and keep a journal on who challenges you the most in each characteristic.

Self control is a tough one. I remember Tina's story of how her step daughter kept putting stickers on some wood in their home, and even after repeatedly asking her to move them, the step daughter was stubbornly leaving them up there. This was a direct affront upon Tina's self control. She could have torn them down and thrown them in the trash. But instead, she confided in her husband, who then took them down and handed them to Tina so that she could then put them up in her step daughter's room in the same order.

I believe that sort of concern and care - even after being tested - is a genuine example of love. Tina exercised patience, as well - more fruit.

These are things our step kids DO see. They remember this.

I have been keeping an album for Lucas for years. I call it his life album. It starts with a picture of Steve and the ex with baby Lucas. It chronicles his sports - his time living there - and his time living with us. He knows the time and love and effort I have put into this album, and he's mentioned how much it means to him that someone is doing that for him. I see it as kindness.

Identify who brings out the best fruit in you - and what fruit it is - why is that?

I believe my girls - ages 5 and 6 - bring out patience in me, something I have always lacked. It's because I want them to learn patience and be better than me! Don't we all, as moms, want our kids to be better than us?

Now, the second part is to identify who you do **not** have that fruit with - who is it? Why? For me, it's my mother in law. She is highly critical of me, and I have difficulty being patient with her when she is criticizing something about me or our family. But that's exactly why God has her in my life! It's easy to be good for people you love!! It's hard to act the "right" way when someone is deliberately hoping you won't!

Being good for people who challenge you is God's way of making us who He needs us to be to bring Him glory.

Now, Identify where fruit is not alive *yet*. Notice I say **YET, because <u>if you continue to walk with God, it *will* be produced within you.</u>**

Galatians 5: 19-21 says "The acts of the sinful nature are obvious; sexual immorality, impurity and debauchery; idolatry and witchcraft; hatred, discord, jealousy, fits of rage, selfish ambition, dissensions, factions and envy; drunkenness, orgies, and the like. I warn you, as I did before, that those who live like this will not inherit the kingdom of God."

Where is the fruit lacking? Do you hate the ex? Do you contribute to dissension?

For me, I needed to identify where I was acting in a provoking manner at times.

For 12 years, when I felt attacked by the ex, I would respond. Email, phone call, letter - any way I could. In doing so, I was *choosing* to participate in negativity and I was *choosing* to provoke her.

It doesn't matter if she was wrong - I still had a duty to God to choose to be godly.

I needed to choose to turn the other cheek, and as I have said, <u>it took me 12 years</u>, but I finally learned how to do that! Don't expect yourself to repair all of your faults overnight!! No matter what is said now, I do not respond. For years, I felt I had to have my say, and defend myself, but I don't have to! Praise God that He set me free from that bondage!

Even in the worst of circumstances, God defends me.

When I stand at the throne, God already knows me. **I don't have any need to stand up at anyone else's throne and defend myself.**

Step moms, tell yourself this:

What they ***THINK*** of me doesn't matter.

What God ***KNOWS*** of me does.

Get to a point with yourself that you can identify these attacks for what they are - it's jealousy against you at times - a wanting you to fail - as Ivana Trump once said, "Success is the best revenge." Step moms, YOU ARE DOING A GOOD THING. YOU ARE DOING A GOOD JOB. Keep doing it, and do it without participating in discord with whomever is trying to lure you into participating in it.

Who do you respect? One person for me is a gal named Gail who always smiled, and when adversity came her way, it could not shake the smile off her face. She handled things calmly and sensibly because she thought first, analyzed quickly - is this a big deal? No - and handled it - she saw good in all things.

Think about someone you respect - what is it about them that you admire? I firmly believe - as long as it is a godly trait- that it's fine to emulate it -

Someone who smiles all the time - walking through the mall or shopping?

Who says hi to strangers?

Gives a compliment to someone they don't know?

Is it someone you know who refuses to take part in gossiping? Or someone who does not participate and instead says kind things or somehow changes the subject?

Someone who doesn't delight in conflict?

I have heard many step moms say they feel the step kids revel in conflict, and we experienced this, too. ***But when we choose to not participate in conflict, it takes the negative excitement out of it for those who are taunting us to participate.***

There is a way to walk away from conflict, to choose to stay still. We don't have to have our say, explain this or that, or be involved in every instance. Once I learned this - again after 12 years!!! - I saw that no matter what was said about me, if I did not participate, it disappeared because God IS in control, and he dissipates the strength of lies and manipulation. If we instead read his Word to the point that we are waking up in the middle of the night remembering scripture, or singing worship songs, then we are victors! If we instead wake up and begin dwelling on what was said to us or about us, we are choosing to live in defeat.

Take off that cloak of desiring protection from lies and false statements, and walk boldly back to the cross where your savior is waiting for you to take His hand and walk with him.

Think about it - if you take a walk with Christ on the beach - are you really going to need to turn to those people who have said things about you and defend yourself? Or stick up for yourself? Or prove how right you are? Or list your accomplishments? No.

You will be calm and content because you are with your groom, and you are His bride.

Remember Christ KNOWS you. What the others THINK of you will be washed away in Christ's blood every time you give it to Him.

Do not hold onto your hurt feelings or they will become more important to you than your walk with Christ.

Cleanse your spirit, and lift your eyes to the Lord. He is shining upon you, smiling down at you, loving you in ways no one on this earth can. He is your defender, your victor, your savior, your protection…

Number 3: Choose to do the right thing **when it is hardest for you.**

Be quiet when others will expect you to defend yourself or get exasperated. Don't pull the silent treatment. Pray and be still in a godly manner. Be aware of the look on your face - make sure it is loving. Ask God to help you be radiant in His eyes, and loving in tough circumstances.

What I am seeing in Lucas now is that he sees clearly who is deliberately trying to cause conflict for others. Sometimes he sees the ex start it with me, or Steve. Sometimes he sees my mother in law start it with the ex, or with Steve, or me. But since I have chosen to no longer participate in the conflict, he no longer sees me as an instigator. In fact, many times he realizes that I haven't participated in verbal conflict with the ex or my mother in law for months, and yet, they criticize me to each other. This happens with many exes who have an alliance with a family member of the dad. Sue's former sister-in-law is best friends with the ex, so she never gives Sue a break. No matter what she does, she is criticized by those two. But as her stepsons got older, they started to realize that the ex and his aunt were jealous of the step mom - listen to this - THE MORE THE STEP MOM REMAINED SILENT! When she defended herself, the boys would sometimes collaborate in the criticism, but when she chose not to defend herself, they found themselves defending her!

That's what's happening with Lucas right now. He knows I have chosen to not speak to the ex because my motives and words are not perceived by her the way I intend. In taking myself out of the equation, God has protected me. And he has used Lucas as part of my shield.

You see, all those times I tried to set the record straight and defend myself, he saw it as me "fighting" not me "fighting back". **We need to be aware of all perceptions, and the damage they do.**

Even when they are confused teens, they see clearly when we are trying to avoid conflict and when we are trying to continue doing good. "Do not grow weary in doing good."

Dwell upon what is good. That means remembering what you have done right. Write it down and remind yourself. My list included helping out financially when I was still in the workforce. I paid for my stepson and his mother to stay in a hotel overnight once. I drove many hours to meet Ann and deliver Lucas to save her money and time.

I always made sure Ann received Mother's Day cards and birthday cards and presents. Even when this wasn't returned to me in kind, *I did it because I wanted Lucas to learn that it mattered.* Now, in college, he does it to both his mom and me, his step mom, because my lesson got through!

And when you are dwelling upon the good, include a list of what the ex has done right! Ann wrote me a letter that I still have. Lucas had lived with us for two years, and the step dad had called me and expressed his compassion for me. He said he and Ann realized Lucas was trying to sabotage me, and that he had tried for years to sabotage him in his marriage to Ann. This was a god incident that united our families! Ann then wrote me a letter, saying, "Thanks for being the mom I can't be right now."

Whatever the reason, try to remember that you are there for that child! No matter what the mom might say, the bottom line is: *She does trust you with her child* or she wouldn't allow him to stay in your care!!! In the hard times, I reminded myself of that, and it mattered. There was never any custody battle over trying to get Lucas back, and that meant she trusted me to mother her son.

Remember that. Even when Lucas asked to move back in with her, after a year of living with us, she told Lucas, "You are a better kid living with them." Ann told Steve the same thing, and again, that was reinforcement that the step mom is doing a good thing!

She often wrote me thank you notes when she would receive a gift I bought for Lucas to mail to her, saying, "Dawn, you are so kind to me."

This won't happen all the time. There were plenty of bad times and bad emails to me, too, and I, unfortunately, responded in kind.

But if we dwell upon the good, write it down and remember it, it can help us remember why we are doing the step mom thing, and why it is working, and why it matters to God!

Number 4: Actively learn to let things go and do good just because it IS good.

When Misty stayed awake all night with her 2 year old stepson and he was throwing up all over her, she focused on loving him, comforting him. She did not focus on the ex and the irritation she might have had that the mother left a very sick child with her.

When the ex is continually late, Tracy could focus on the irritation of that continually making her schedule difficult. Instead, she focuses on loving her stepsons and encouraging them that their mom will be there. That is choosing to do good.

When Brittany takes her step daughter, Alyssa, to all of her activities and church, she could become bitter that she is doing the "mom's work", but instead she is exercising LOVE, and doing the right thing, the good thing, for the child.

For a long time, I was bitter that I did so much for Lucas, and the ex did not. I wanted to do it, but I still felt taken advantage of.

When I finally admitted that to God (Which He already knew!!!!) he took that feeling away from me. And the funny thing was, as God released that bitterness from my heart, I felt a forgiveness toward the ex wash over me. Then, people started saying more and more things to me, expressing appreciation for what I did for Lucas and his sports teams, recognizing that I was there, and how tough it was at times to drag two babies with me!

But you see, that's how good God is. He knew I desired earthly VOCAL appreciation, and once I submitted that desire to him, and laid it at the foot of the cross, he gave me that appreciation from people that had seen me at sports games for years, and suddenly felt the need to compliment me about it! God is so good. **He knows us so intimately, and He does desire to love upon us in ways that are very much the ways we DO understand.**

What has he done to love on you?

Number 5: DO NOT GOSSIP.

Another thing that is challenging in the step mom and ex relationship is gossip. Nearly every step mom and ex I have met engage in gossip. This is a very mighty serpent to crush. Every ex wants to tell people that the step mom is not as good as she is, and every step mom wants to tell her people that the ex is not as good as she is.

When we conquer that, we will be set free.

People will love and respect you for what you say and do, not what you try to convince them of.

Many step moms waste a lot of their time talking to their friends and family about what the ex has done, said, or not done. They then list the many things they have done above and beyond what the mother has done. I was certainly guilty of this.

I truly believe God wants us to be set free from the stronghold of gossip.

When he finally loosed the chains on me from that, I was amazed at how little I cared about what the ex or my mother in law were saying behind my back, because by being obedient, and choosing NOT to gossip, God not only stopped my behavior, but he set me free from even caring what others were saying about me.

Again, who cares what someone THINKS of you when God KNOWS you??????

It simply doesn't matter what someone says about you or what you have done or why you have done it, because the absolute bottom line is GOD KNOWS EXACTLY WHAT YOU DID AND WHY YOU DID IT. If your motives are right and in line with his will, HE is the only one who matters.

When you feel yourself welling up inside and wanting to say something, contemplate why you think you need to say it? Are you feeling slighted, betrayed, attacked? Will talking about it really help?

If so, get therapy with a Christian therapist who can guide you to healing, not the self satisfaction of telling someone off, or considering it.

When you get tired, or attacked, or irritated, sit down right away and read the Word. Read Psalms - any of them! Put on worship music - but **take godly control of the sinful nature that is trying to take control of you!**

You can do this. We face some big battles as step moms, and most of them are based on false statements about us or false impressions of us.

Be Still.
Be Loved.
Be Strong.

You are a step mom because GOD KNEW YOU COULD HANDLE IT. He knew you could do it. He knew you would be victorious.

Be strong. Take courage. God is with you.

Number 5: Identify those destructive behaviors within you that are causing you pain and stop them.

No one feels good after gossiping, if they are in line with Jesus Christ. If you are walking with Him, you will feel guilty after you gossip to someone about the ex, or about your step kids, or your in laws.

You will feel yucky.

I started to realize this, and when I actively started to DELIBERATELY not say negative things about any of them, I felt clean - I WAS SPIRITUALLY CLEANSED!

I broke that stronghold.

I no longer need to shout from the mountaintops what has been said about me or to me. I have complete confidence that every time something is whispered that is not godly, guess what? GOD HEARS IT. GOD KNOWS IT. HE WILL HANDLE THAT ATTACK IN WAYS YOU DON'T UNDERSTAND AND IN WAYS YOU DON'T NEED TO WORRY ABOUT.

He takes care of us. He loves us. "Cast your burdens upon the Lord and He will sustain you!"

Is your stronghold the irritated feeling when the step kids don't act like they are cadets responding to your requests to help around the house?

Try telling a joke to them after - or before - you request something. Maybe your request is coming across as "too bossy". It won't hurt any of us to try a little more kindness and patience, will it?

Or try, "hey, I was thinking we could go get ice cream after you put those clothes away."

Think about how you would want someone to treat and talk to your kids if they were the step kids.

Understand and accept that all step children - all children - lie. They have many emotions and hurts that they don't understand and in Lucas' case, he sometimes wanted so badly to be the center of attention in whatever group he was in, that he lied to have the center stage. When I sit back and think of all the lies he's told to the ex and my in laws, it's amazing they haven't put a hit out on me! But Lucas, like most step kids, was angry his parents were divorced, was sad he couldn't have them at the same time, felt guilty that he loves me, felt he was betraying his "real" parents if he said something nice about me…. It goes on and on.

Yes, adults should realize this is going on. But many want to believe it based on their own insecurities or issues. That's another book for another time!!

Number 6: Make sure your trust is in GOD.

We can sometimes lean too much on our men, or our friends, or even ourselves. We need to have an *intimate* relationship with God. Our trust needs to be in Him wholly.

If it's in ourselves, we will fulfill that need to have our say.

If it's in our men, they will disappoint us.

If it's in God, we can sit back and watch Him work all things together for good, for those who love the Lord, and work according to His purpose.

Number 7: Realize that this is ALL a spiritual battle NOT an earthly one!

Ephesians 6:12 "For our struggle is not against **flesh** and **blood**, but against the rulers, against the authorities, against the powers of this dark world and against the spiritual forces of evil in the heavenly realms."

The ex, the in laws, the step kids, your husband - they are NOT your enemy. Make your mindset clear. THIS IS A SPIRITUAL BATTLE.

And we are ALREADY victorious!

Romans 8:28 - 39 "And we know that in all things God works for the good of those who love him, who have been called according to his purpose. For those God foreknew he also predestined to be conformed to the image of his Son, that he might be the firstborn among many brothers and sisters. And those he predestined, he also called; those he called, he also justified; those he justified, he also glorified. What, then, shall we say in response to these things? **If God is for us, who can be against us?** He who did not spare his own Son, but gave him up for us all—how will he not also, along with him, graciously give us all things? Who will bring any charge against those whom God has chosen? It is God who justifies. **Who then can condemn?**

No one. Christ Jesus who died—more than that, who was raised to life—is at the right hand of God and is also interceding for us. Who shall separate us from the love of Christ? Shall trouble or hardship or persecution or famine or nakedness or danger or sword? As it is written:

"For your sake we face death all day long;

we are considered as sheep to be slaughtered."

No, in all these things we are more than conquerors through him who loved us. For I am convinced that neither death nor life, neither angels nor demons, neither the present nor the future, nor any powers, neither height nor depth, nor anything else in all creation, will be able to separate us from the love of God that is in Christ Jesus our Lord."

Step moms, God loves you.

He loves you in such a mighty way that you don't yet fully understand the strength and dedication of that love.

*And HE will **never** stop proving it to you!*

CPSIA information can be obtained
at www.ICGtesting.com
Printed in the USA
BVHW050057060122
625206BV00007B/657